Scripture to Live By

*True Stories and Spiritual
Lessons Inspired by the
Word of God*

EDITED BY ARRON CHAMBERS

ADAMS MEDIA
AVON, MASSACHUSETTS

Published by
Adams Media, an F+W Publications Company
57 Littlefield Street
Avon, MA 02322
www.adamsmedia.com

Unless otherwise noted, Scripture quotations are taken from the
Holy Bible: New International Version. Copyright © 1973, 1978, 1984
by International Bible Society. Used by permission of Zondervan
Publishing House. All rights reserved.

ISBN 10: 1-59869-065-5
ISBN 13: 978-1-59869-065-1

Printed in the United States of America

J I H G F E D C B A

Library of Congress Cataloging-in-Publication Data
is available from the publisher.

This publication is designed to provide accurate and authoritative information with
regard to the subject matter covered. It is sold with the understanding that the publisher is not engaged in rendering legal, accounting, or other professional advice. If
legal advice or other expert assistance is required, the services of a competent professional person should be sought.
—From a *Declaration of Principles* jointly adopted by a Committee of the American Bar
Association and a Committee of Publishers and Associations

Many of the designations used by manufacturers and sellers to distinguish their prod-
uct are claimed as trademarks. Where those designations appear in this book and
Adams Media was aware of a trademark claim, the designations have been printed
with initial capital letters.

This book is available at quantity discounts for bulk purchases.
For information, please call 1-800-289-0963.

Contents

For my mom,
     Linda Chambers.

You are not just my mom. You are my hero,
my encourager, my teacher, my example, and
my friend. I love how you love God, and how
you love me and my family. You've made each
day of my life wondrous.

Acknowledgments

My wife, Rhonda, and my children, Ashton, Levi, Sylas, and Payton—thanks for all you did to help me finish this book. I could not have done this without you—nor would I have wanted to. I cherish every second with you.

Dr. Roger and Linda Chambers, my parents—I grew to love the Scriptures as I watched you live them each day of my childhood. Thank you for taking the Scriptures off of the shelf and placing them in my heart.

The contributors—thank you for your stories and your willingness to share them with others. I was so blessed by them—even if your story was not included in this book. I loved working with you on this project. You are professionals, all.

Twila Sias and Kim Boyd—I can't thank you enough for all you did to help me finish this book. With you at my side, I knew not even a hurricane could stop us. You are amazing women. Thanks for being Christ to me.

Tamela Hancock Murray, my agent—I'm so glad that you are my partner in this ministry. Thank you for encouraging me, advising me, and representing me with such class and professionalism.

Paula Munier, Andrea Norville, and the Adams Media team—thanks for giving me a chance to work with you on this project. I'm so grateful for your patience and for your commitment to excellence.

My church family and the team at Christ's Church—it is an honor to be associated with people like you. Your love, faith, and eternal optimism bring unspeakable joy to my ministry.

Introduction

The Bible was not a prop in our home when I was a child. We didn't leave it out on a table to be seen by guests, or on a shelf to collect dust. No, the Bible was the foundation for everything we did. We believed the Scriptures were the very words of God. Mom and Dad read them with us, to us, and in our presence. They went to the Bible with questions, and shared with us its answers.

My parents believed in the power of God's word to teach us, guide us, and protect us, so they surrounded us with the Scriptures. The Bible was not a book we lived with, but a book we lived by.

That's why I was so excited when I was presented an opportunity to help write and edit this book, *Scripture to Live By*. This book is a collection of true and interesting stories I've gathered from twenty-nine different authors. I intentionally sought out authors of all ages and from various backgrounds. This book includes stories from college students and professors, church leaders, preachers, comedians, missionaries, musicians, teachers, business leaders, university and seminary presidents, soldiers, retirees, moms, and dads.

It includes stories of love, survival, and hope. These stories will make you laugh, cry, remember, and think about your life. I hope that the time you spend with this book will lead to countless blessings. It's my prayer that this book itself will be a lasting blessing to your life, so I've designed this book to connect these twenty-nine true stories with the true stories from two other authors: God and you.

Each story in this book is followed by a devotion written by me and a call to action designed to connect the author's story, God's story, and yours. It's my prayer that your life will be blessed as you read these stories and apply the lessons from God's Scriptures to your life.

When I turned thirteen, my Dad gave me a Bible. In the front cover he wrote: "This book will create in you the good, the true, and the beautiful." As you journey with this book on the path with God one wondrous day at a time, I pray these stories, God's story, and yours will fill your life with goodness, truth, and beauty.

Blessings,
Arron

Spring Always Comes

By Kim Jackson

What shall we say, then? Shall we go on sinning so that grace may increase? By no means! We died to sin; how can we live in it any longer? Or don't you know that all of us who were baptized into Christ Jesus were baptized into his death? We were therefore buried with him through baptism into death in order that, just as Christ was raised from the dead through the glory of the Father, we too may live a new life.

—ROMANS 6:1–4

"That's odd," I thought, as I walked through the front yard of my Midwest home. "It looks like something's trying to grow up right outside my bedroom window."

I bent over to take a closer look. "How weird! Not only is something that I didn't plant growing there, whatever it is, they're lined up in as perfect a row as you're ever going to see. Strange!"

1

Intrigued, I made it a habit to walk around the outside of my house each evening when the weather permitted. We'd had a rough winter in Illinois, and it had started far too early for my liking. It didn't help that my personal life seemed to mirror the season. After months of gray sky outside and dark mood inside, I was looking forward to saying that spring had sprung.

A few weeks into my walk-around-the-house-in-the-evening routine, I realized that the mystery plants growing so perfectly outside my bedroom window were tulips. "I'm pretty sure there is no such thing as volunteer tulips," I said to a friend one day. "But how in the world did a row of tulip bulbs get planted right under my nose without me knowing about it?"

As the weather warmed up, so did my spirits. I began to believe that the icy season in my heart was going to melt away even as the sun's rays made puddles where the neighbor kid's snowman used to be.

But even as I dared to hope, phone calls and e-mails reminded me of both a relationship careening out of control and mounting financial difficulties. Discouraged, I slumped on the couch and buried my head in a pillow. *God, I'm so tired. Is this season ever going to end?* Depressed and drained of energy, I got up off the couch just long enough to get ready for bed. I caught my reflection in the bathroom mirror. *Good grief, even my face looks gray.*

Sleep was a great escape. I didn't have to face the realities of my circumstances if I never got out of bed, right? When my alarm went off the next morning, I hit the snooze button. Once. Twice. Three times.

Oh, but responsibilities beckoned. I sat up and sighed . . . at least it looked like the sun was shining. That was a plus. As I opened the blinds of my bedroom window, I saw a splash of color. I spoke out loud: "Oh, my goodness, the tulips have opened!"

Grabbing a jacket, I jogged out the front door and around the corner. And there they were: a perfect row of the most glorious, vibrant red tulips I've ever seen. "Oh, Lord, these are marvelous! What a colorful, wonderful gift."

I knelt down in the dew-soaked grass and extended my hand to touch one of the brand-new blossoms sitting atop a stem that seemed exceptionally tall. I traced the graceful lines of the deep, cup-shaped blossom. What artistry! And the color! The shade of red was absolutely eye popping. "These tulips are amazing," I said aloud as I stood to my feet. "Simply amazing."

My spirits were buoycd by the tulip display. The challenges of the workday seemed to fade as I remembered the colorful surprise that had greeted my morning. I was excited to share my big news, so I called a friend and we met for coffee and a walk around the park.

"The mystery tulips bloomed today! Oh, and they are the most vivid red I've ever seen! And they're so tall! I can't begin to do them justice by describing them—you'll just have to see them for yourself. I still don't have a clue how they showed up in my yard, but I'm sure glad they did."

With that, Heather laughed. "Finally! Now I can tell you the rest of the story."

"What? You were in on this?"

"Yes, I confess . . . but I wasn't alone."

"What do you mean?"

"Well, I had the idea. But I didn't pay for the tulip bulbs."

"I don't understand."

Heather smiled. "Sit back, Kim, and enjoy your coffee. I'll tell you the whole story. It began last November. Remember when you went to the retreat in Indiana?"

"Sure. How could I forget that weekend? When I tried to leave, my car doors were frozen shut! We had such a bad storm on my way home that I prayed nonstop."

"Yes, that's the weekend I'm talking about. The Friday you left, I went to the store and picked out the tulip bulbs. I used money from your Fun Fund to pay for them, so Sandy and Deb were co-conspirators, if you will."

I shook my head. So I had been blessed by Kim's Fun Fund yet again. Deb and Sandy, my friends in Florida, knew I had been going through a challenging season, so they had sent money to my friend Heather in Illinois, with instructions to use the funds to encourage me. Heather had been faithfully and creatively blessing me out of the Fun Fund for months. The first installment came after I endured a particularly painful confrontation in my professional life. The next day Heather had called with an invitation to dine at my favorite Italian restaurant, with the tab being picked up by Kim's Fun Fund, of course. A month later, after I had been out of state for a week helping chaperone hundreds of teenagers at a conference, I was greeted with a balloon bouquet on my kitchen table when I returned home.

"So, Kim's Fun Fund strikes again?"

"Indeed it has. And once I knew you had driven out of town, I arrived at your house with the bulbs and my gardening tools. Down on my knees outside your bedroom window, I dropped each bulb into its cozy winter home, spread dirt over each one, and said a little prayer. The timing for your being away from home coincided perfectly with my hope that if I planted the bulbs then, they would bloom near Easter. It just seemed right for the bulbs to 'resurrect' at that time.

The only concern I had was that you might notice that someone had been digging in your front yard, but God already had a plan in mind."

"He did?"

"The storm. God delivered an early winter storm . . . and all the traces of my digging up your yard were covered by snow—just in time. When you pulled in your driveway Sunday evening there was nary a trace of my—literal—dirty work."

"So let me get this straight: you had the tulip idea, you used money sent from my friends in Florida to fund the project, you secretly planted the bulbs while I was away, and then God covered your tracks in the form of a snowstorm. So . . . you've spent all winter knowing that in a few months the mystery tulips would bloom to bless and encourage me. Wow . . . I feel loved!"

"That was the idea. You've been so discouraged—gone through some winter months of your own, so to speak. But spring always comes, Kim. Spring always comes."

Spring always comes. Heather's words resonated in my weary soul. I tried to imagine what the tulip bulbs looked like on the chilly November day when they were dropped in the ground outside my bedroom window. What words would describe them? Ugly, underground, and unknown. Yet after the cold spell required for the tulips to grow, they had transformed into beautiful, bold blessings. Both the harsh winter weather as well as the welcome spring sun were necessary for the tulips to complete their upward journey.

Heather interrupted my thoughtful silence. "Oh, and Kim, there's one more thing. There are dozens and dozens of tulip varieties available. But I chose yours with special care. Yours are called Kingsblood. Happy Easter, Kim."

✝ The Pastor Says . . .

I don't have a green thumb. I don't even have a green pinky. Plants have a picture of me on the wall of their post offices. Why? I kill plants on a regular basis. This is not intentional. I'm just not a very good gardener.

My brother-in-law, on the other hand, is a fantastic gardener. He can actually put tomato seeds in the ground, and tomato plants grow that actually produce tomatoes. Can you believe that? I can't, because when I put seeds in the ground, dirt grows. Nothing happens, and that's how it should be. That's how God designed the process.

Put a seed in the ground and, in the hidden realm of worms, dirt, moisture, and darkness, a transformation occurs that unleashes intended potential. God intends for seeds to become plants. That's what seeds were designed to do. Unplanted seeds are destined to always be . . . seeds. Unplanted seeds will never know the pleasure of sunshine on their leaves. Unplanted seeds will never know the joy of blooming. Unplanted seeds will never experience the pleasure of providing nourishment and pleasure to others. Unplanted seeds will never know the pleasure of being a tulip and the pleasure of being seen as an expression of God's faithfulness.

I want to remind you that two important things occur when seeds are planted: death and life.

When a seed is planted in the ground a death of identity occurs—while beneath the surface the seed dies to itself and becomes not seed. But life occurs as a plant pushes up through the dirt reaching for the nourishment of the sun.

For all of these reasons—and for others we may not fully understand with minds familiar only with the modern approach to horticulture—the Apostle Paul compares being baptized to being planted. In Romans 6:5, Paul, when describing what happens at baptism, uses a word that is only used one time in the Bible and that word means "planted." This is how verse 5 literally reads: "If we have been *planted* with him like this in his death, we will certainly also be united with him in his resurrection" (emphasis mine).

At my baptism, in the spring of 1978, I too, was planted. At your baptism you were planted. At our baptisms, you and I experienced death and life. When we were beneath the surface, like a seed, we died to ourselves and became new. As we came up out of the water, our intended potential was realized. We emerged as new creations, with a new life, and new identity.

I hope you never look at tulips and baptismal services the same way again.

—Arron Chambers

Spiritual Lessons in Action

Buy some flower seeds and plant them someplace where their blooming will be a reminder that spring always comes.

A Banquet for the 912th

By Marc Imboden

T hen the LORD said, "I will surely return to you about this time next year, and Sarah your wife will have a son." Now Sarah was listening at the entrance to the tent, which was behind him. Abraham and Sarah were already old and well advanced in years, and Sarah was past the age of child-bearing. So Sarah laughed to herself as she thought, "After I am worn out and my master is old, will I now have this pleasure?" Then the LORD said to Abraham, "Why did Sarah laugh and say, 'Will I really have a child, now that I am old?' Is anything too hard for the LORD? I will return to you at the appointed time next year and Sarah will have a son." Sarah was afraid, so she lied and said, "I did not laugh." But he said, "Yes, you did laugh."

—GENESIS 18:10—15

I'm sure that you've read some great war stories from World War II, Vietnam, Desert Storm, and even more recently from Iraq. You know . . . the kind with action, adventure, and bloodshed? Well, this is not one of those kinds of stories. This is a story of unexpected blessings.

I was stationed in the Persian Gulf with the 912th MASH Army reserve unit from November 1990 through August 1991. During this tumultuous time, a lot of unexpected things happened.

We landed in Dhahran, Saudi Arabia, the night Iraq started sending SCUD missiles into that country. I remember getting off the plane in the middle of the night, hauling my duffel bag and gear, and being shuffled off to a nearby rat-infested warehouse that we were told would be our quarters. When we entered the warehouse, there was a sea of olive drab bodies occupying every square inch of the floor. Exhausted from traveling for the last thirty-some hours, I tried to find a spot to roll out my sleeping bag. When I finally lay down an hour later for what I thought would be a long-overdue nap, sirens from every direction started blaring. Immediately, I was jolted into a state of alertness unlike anything I had ever experienced, as I heard soldiers all around me yelling, "Gas! Gas! Gas!"

Donning my gas mask and chemical-protective gear, I remember thinking, "My first night at war, and I'm gonna die." Running outside with the other panic-stricken soldiers, I looked up just in time to see the method of my execution: a SCUD missile headed directly toward us.

As my life flashed before my eyes, suddenly, and quite unexpectedly, what looked like a bottle rocket, but was really a Patriot missile, came out of nowhere and knocked the SCUD out of its path and into oblivion. The cheers were short-lived, as the next SCUD could be seen right behind the first one. Again I thought, "I'm gonna die," but then another Patriot missile saved the day.

This went on for several days. This was no way to live, expecting the worst, but this was our reality.

Eventually, duty called, and we were set up as a humanitarian mission in an abandoned hospital in Kuwait City. Our life in the hospital started to feel the slightest bit normal—if normal is even a possibility in a wartime situation.

We started to perform our duties during shift work and actually had some time off. During this time off, the Army let us go into town every once in a while for a little R and R. So, where do a bunch of Americans go in a foreign city when they have a little break? The mall, of course! So, off to the mall we went.

Now, the malls in Kuwait are called malls, but that's where the similarities end. The malls in Kuwait have no Chick-fil-As, Foot Locker shoe stores, multiplex cinemas, or any of the other quintessential, homogenized American boutiques that we've grown so accustomed to. These malls were extravagant, and this particular mall was spectacularly grand!

It was constructed entirely of marble . . . I'm talking marble floors, marble walls, marble ceilings, marble benches, and marble bathrooms complete with marble bidets.

The front doors of the mall were at least fifteen feet tall and completely covered in gold leaf. The first floor was composed entirely of silver shops. The jewelry was so bright that we actually put on our sunglasses wherever we went on the first floor. I've never seen so much silver jewelry in my entire life. The second level was . . . you guessed it . . . gold. Every window of every shop was filled with every type of gold jewelry imaginable. It really did hurt your eyes a little. The top floor had every kind of exotic stone (diamonds, rubies, emeralds, etc.) you could ever want or need—not that any of us were in need of any jewelry—nevertheless, it was there for the haggling.

All of that opulence was making us kind of hungry, so we decided to look for some authentic Kuwaiti food. There was, of course, your standard variety of McDonald's, KFC, and Burger King fast-food chains, but we wanted to experience the culture. I have found that you can travel to the most remote corner of the globe, and still find a Big Mac or a Whopper. This would not do, however, so we left the sparkly mall to venture into the city and find authentic food.

On our way out the front door, a Kuwaiti man, looking very much like every other Kuwaiti man, dressed in the traditional long white robe and white headdress, stopped us to thank us for leaving our families and homes and coming all this way to help his people. We, of course, did the "Aw, shucks!" routine and denied any real heroism, stating that we really didn't do anything, but he kept shaking our hands insisting that he must find a way to thank us. Was there anything he could do for us?

I half-jokingly asked, "Could you tell us where to find the best Kuwaiti food?"

His eyes lit up and he said, "Ah . . . that would be my house."

Instinctively, we told him, "No, that really won't be necessary," but he was very persistent and kept asking us when we could come. The three of us sort of looked at each other and said, "How about next Saturday?"

He jumped up a little and said, "Excellent! You bring four more of your friends and meet me here at noon on Saturday."

Not really expecting that this man would show up, let alone cook for seven of us, we sort of shrugged it off and went back to the hospital. That next Saturday, we collected our four other friends and drove to the mall, not expecting the nice Kuwaiti man to really be there, but, to our amazement, there he stood! It was exactly 12:00 noon, and he was there waiting for us with a fleet of four long black limousines, all with chauffeurs at the ready.

As it turns out, this guy was the owner of said sparkly mall, as well as a few other sparkly malls, and not only had he not forgotten about our little food pact, he was seriously excited, and it appeared, he was almost giddy.

We all awkwardly climbed into the cars to find that these were not the rental limos from prom night; these were the real deal, with cold champagne waiting for us, and televisions tuned to CNN. After a short drive through town, we found ourselves at yet another huge, sparkly establishment, and, although it was as big as a mall, this was no mall. Now, I've been to my fair share of really nice houses in America—even a few mansions and estates, but nothing can really prepare you for walking into someone's palace. And again with the marble; I mean the whole place, top to bottom, was marble. There was an indoor Olympic-sized marble swimming pool, two grand curved staircases—completely made of marble. The bizarreness of the whole situation must have been obvious on our faces, as we just kept murmuring, "Wow!"

He then led us into the parlor, a giant (marble, of course) room with what was most likely the largest Persian rug in the known universe; it looked like a small football field. The only other items in the room were pillows . . . lots and lots of pillows. I'd say there were about two hundred pillows lining the perimeter of this *Guinness Book of World Records* nominee for the world's largest rug. He called this the "Tea Room" and, sitting in the Tea Room, were seven of his friends sitting on pillows, sipping tea from tiny cups, and waiting for our arrival.

As he introduced us to this small group of friends, I realized that this group represented a sort of microcosm of contemporary Kuwaiti culture. There was a doctor, an engineer, a journalist, a restaurant owner, a lawyer, a professor, and his brother, who was part owner of the sparkly mall franchise. It was becoming apparent to me as we sat for tea and conversation that this man went out of his way not only to let us experience a Kuwaiti dinner, but also to encounter a much broader cultural picture.

After tea, he announced that it was time for dinner and led us into one of the largest dining rooms—or, I should say, dining halls—I've ever seen. The huge, hand-carved dining table looked like it belonged in the Ming Dynasty era, and came complete with high-backed, hand-carved chairs to go all the way around it. He then rang a small bell. Women who had been busy in the kitchen started bringing out the platters of food.

Now, up to this point, I know that this story might seem a bit fictionalized, or a little embellished at the very least, but I can promise you that it's not. However, if you thought that the story so far was unbelievable, the next part is gonna kill ya.

There were about six or seven women—the host's mother, his wife, several sisters, and a few sisters in-law—bringing out the food. Each woman carried two large platters of some Kuwaiti delicacy, which added up to about fourteen main courses! Keep in mind that there were only fifteen of us there.

It gets better. As soon as the ladies put down the platters, they turned around and went back to the kitchen, only to return with another armful of main courses. Our jaws dropped once again. One more trip to the kitchen yielded several more platters of main courses, desserts, and finally the "coup de grâce": a large American-style pepperoni pizza.

Our host just smiled and said, "You guys said that you wanted to try some authentic Kuwaiti food, so I had my mother and family make every Kuwaiti dish we could think of. And just in case you couldn't find something you like, there's pizza." I counted thirty-nine dishes, not including the pizza.

I've been on several mission trips (you know the scene) where you're sitting at some really sweet host's dinner table with a mouth full of some mystery meat, smiling and nodding but not really swallowing, saying how delicious it is, while the whole time you're trying to figure out what kind of monkey or marsupial you're eating. Well, we were definitely not in that situation.

We ate and ate and ate. All thirty-nine dishes were incredible. We ate with our hands (customary in the Middle East), told stories, laughed, and exchanged histories and ideas. I think we ate for over five hours, stopping every once in a while to stretch.

At the end of this amazing culinary and cultural experience we said good-bye to our new friends, thanked our host over and over, told the women in the kitchen how incredible everything was, and climbed back into the stretch limos to return to planet Earth. When I had asked, "Could you tell us where to find the best Kuwaiti food?" I had expected directions to a Kuwaiti restaurant, but what I got was an afternoon full of unexpected blessings.

✝ *The Pastor Says* . . .

Some of life's sweetest blessings are unexpected.

Your boss sticks her head into your office and with a smile says, "Good job on that presentation today."

A check tumbles out of a birthday card.

A friend offers to buy your lunch.

A dozen roses wait for you on the kitchen table when you come downstairs after putting the kids to bed.

You stumble through your front door after a long day at work only to be greeted by your friends and family shouting, "Surprise!"

After years of trying, you finally give up all hope of first steps, a first birthday party, midnight feedings in a rocking chair, and PTA, only to find yourself holding a positive pregnancy test in your forty-one-year-old fingers.

A knock at the door announces that your in-laws are in town for an unannounced weeklong visit. Well, maybe this doesn't qualify, but you get the point.

God loves to send unexpected blessings when we least expect them. Just ask Abraham and Sarah. Abram and Sarai were living a quiet life in Haran. Things in their life to this point had not gone as expected. They expected to go to Canaan, but they found themselves living with Abram's father in Haran. They expected to have children, but Sarai was barren; she was unable to conceive. They expected to live out their lives in Haran, but God called them to leave everything—their country, their people, their father's household—and set out for Canaan. They expected to keep the names they were given at birth— who wouldn't—but God changed their names to Abraham and Sarah.

God announced to Abraham that he and Sarah would have a son and that their descendants would be as numerous as the stars in the heavens. When Sarah heard about this plan she did what any other ninety-year-old barren woman would do— she laughed. And you can't blame her. In what universe can a

ninety-year-old barren women expect to experience the blessing of having a child?

Answer: God's universe. We were created by a God who
loves to give us unexpected blessings, and He expects us to
expect them.

The only person more surprised than Sarah during this
unexpected announcement is none other than the Lord. I
expected Sarah to be surprised, but I did not expect the Lord to
be surprised by Sarah's reaction. God seems a little offended by
Sarah's laughter.

Sarah laughs and the Lord turns to Abraham and asks, "Why
did Sarah laugh and say, 'Will I really have a child, now that I
am old?'" (Gen. 18:13). God then asks a question He only asks
twice in the entire Bible (Gen. 18:14; Jer. 32:27): "Is anything too
hard for the Lord?"

Answer: No.

Your health problems are not too hard for the Lord.

Your financial problems are not too hard for the Lord.

Your family problems are not too hard for the Lord.

Don't lose heart. Don't give up. Don't laugh.

God loves to give His children unexpected blessings.

God wants to bless you unexpectedly—expect it.

—Arron Chambers

Spiritual Lessons in Action

List the top five challenges you are facing today. After each
challenge I want you to write the following question and
answer: "Is anything too hard for the Lord?" "No."

God Bless Dad . . . Again

By Paula Munier

Two are better than one, because they have a good return for their work. . . . .
——ECCLESIASTES 4:9

Every night when Sarah put Joey to bed, she prompted him to say his prayers. He was only eight, so his prayers were typically short.

"God bless Dad," he always began, "and Mom and Grandpa and Grandma and Mrs. Harper, my teacher, and Charlie, my best friend, and, uh, amen."

"Amen." Sarah would hug him tight and tuck him in. He'd be out in minutes and sleep soundly until she roused him in the morning. But tonight was different.

"Time for prayers," she told Joey as she did each evening when he scampered into bed.

"Do we have to?" Joey turned away from Sarah and tucked his arm over his head so she couldn't see his face.

Sarah laughed. "Yes, we have to."

"Can't we skip it, just this once?" Joey's voice was muffled.

"There's no skipping God," Sarah said. She sat down on the edge of the bed to wait him out. After a couple of minutes, Joey sat up. "All right, but I'm not praying for Dad anymore."

"I see," said Sarah, which was how she tried to answer every comment regarding her ex-husband. They had divorced nearly a year ago. For Sarah, it meant that she could finally feel safe again, and for Joey, it meant that he could love his father without worrying about his mother. He stayed at home with Sarah during the week and visited his dad on the weekends.

She prided herself on saying as little as possible about Joe Senior, since she didn't have much good to say. She didn't blame Joey; Sarah wasn't praying for his dad, either, but she was praying about him. That was the best she could do, at least for now.

Apparently it was the best Joey could do, too.

Joey folded his stubby little fingers into each other. "God bless Mom and Grandpa and Grandma and Mrs. Harper, my teacher, and Charlie, my best friend, and, uh, amen."

"Amen." Sarah hugged Joey, and he burst into tears. She took him onto her lap and rocked him until his sobs subsided. Finally she asked. "What happened?"

"I can't be a scout any more." He looked at her with sad, reddened eyes.

"What? What do you mean?"

"Dad says that since Nathan and Tyler aren't in the Scouts, I can't be either."

The month before Joe Senior had moved in with his girlfriend, Jennifer. She had twin boys Joey's age, Nathan and Tyler. Joe Senior had cut his weekly visits with Joey to every other weekend—the same weekends the twins were with him and Jennifer. On the weekends when the twins visited with their father, Joey stayed home with Sarah. Joe Senior and Jennifer liked their time alone. So when he was with his dad, Joey found himself competing for his attention with Nathan and Tyler—and he didn't like it.

"I have to do what they do." He frowned. "Basketball."

Apparently the twins were grammar-school giants. They towered over Joey—and every other kid in the third grade. "So? I can take you if your father can't do it." *Or won't*, she thought.

"I need Dad." Joey wiped his tears with the back of his hand and sniffed. "He's supposed to help me with the Pinewood Derby."

Sarah had no idea what the Pinewood Derby was. She had never been a Boy Scout. "Anything he can do, I can do better."

Joey giggled. "Yeah, right." He giggled again. "You have to take a block of wood and carve it into a race car, Mom."

Carve. Sarah thought for a moment. "I can carve a turkey. I can carve a pumpkin. I can carve a heart out of ice."

"No way."

"I did it once—for a prom back in high school. I think I can handle a little car."

"I don't know, Mom. You need tools and stuff. Like Dad's." Joey's voice broke. "Last year Dad helped me carve this really cool car. We painted it blue."

Joe Sr. was a weekend carpenter, with lots of tools he'd charged on Sarah's Sears card while they were married. She was still paying the card off—while the tools languished in Jennifer's three-car garage.

"We'll get whatever we need at the hardware store." She gave him a hug. "It'll be fun! Now, back to sleep."

"You're dreaming, Mom."

"Quiet now." Sarah sat by her son until he fell asleep, praying for the Pinewood Derby.

The next day was Saturday. Sarah drove Joey down to the official Boy Scout store to pick up the official Pinewood Derby block of wood, which was heavy as a brick and just as uninspired. Then they went to the hardware store, where Sarah spent all her mad money on handsaws, glue, carving knives, sandpaper, whittling books, paint, and stickers. She and Joey searched the Internet for directions, reading up on aerodynamics, preferred weights and shapes, and the best way to build the fastest cars. They printed out pictures of previous Pinewood Derby winners from across the country. These sleek race cars bore no resemblance to the block of wood before them.

"I told you it wasn't going to be easy, Mom." Joey sat in the kitchen with a carving knife in one hand and the block in another. He looked at the design they'd decided upon—a gleaming silver bullet on four wheels—then looked back at the wooden block. "Here goes."

He took the knife and shaved a miniscule sliver off one side of the block. And another. And another. Twenty minutes and barely an eighteenth of an inch later, he put down the block and said, "Your turn, Mom. I'm going to watch TV."

How long could this take? Sarah thought, and took over the whittling. It was hard work, and her fingers ached. Then her thumb slipped, and the knife sliced into the palm of her hand. "Ouch!" Sarah dropped the block, grabbed a paper towel, and ran for the Band-Aids. Joey came running after her.

"Are you all right?"

"I'm fine."

"I told you we couldn't do it, Mom. We need Dad."

Sarah held her breath, then let it out slowly. *We do not need that man,* she thought, but aloud she said, "We're not through yet."

"Mom, we have to take it in to get weighed tomorrow. The race is the day after that. It'll take forever to carve it. And you're bleeding, Mom."

"I'm fine." She wrapped her hand in gauze and, with Joey's help, secured it with several Band-Aids. "See? Good as new. Come on, we've got work to do."

Back in the kitchen, Sarah and Joey stared at the block. "What we lack in craft, we'll make up for in imagination," Sarah said.

"What?"

"We need an idea." Sarah shuffled through their printouts of past Pinewood Derby winners. "Some of these aren't carved much at all. Look, here's one cut to look like a vampire's coffin."

Joey giggled. "That's funny. They painted it black and everything."

"Okay, so what else is shaped like this? What else comes in blocks?"

Joey thought about it. "Bricks."

"Concrete."

"Ice."

"Ice! That's brilliant!" Sarah kissed Joey. "You're my little genius!"

"What did I say?"

"Go get that diorama you made for your book report."

"The one with the penguins?"

"Yes." Sarah grinned. "Go on, go get it!"

While Joey fetched the diorama, Sarah said a quick prayer. "Please let this work, God. I'm no Boy Scout."

The diorama was half a cardboard box lined with aluminum foil "ice." The sides were painted blue. On top of the silver "glacier" were wind-up plastic penguins from the toy store—a scene from a children's book called *Penguins on Ice.*

"I don't get it, Mom."

"Sure you do." Sarah placed one of the little plastic penguins on the block of wood.

"Paint the block white, and what do you have?"

Joey grinned. "An iceberg!"

"Exactly!" Sarah pointed to the box of model paints. "Start painting!"

By the next morning they were finished. Joey had painted the block and attached the wheels. Together they glued on five of the little penguins.

"It looks stupid." Joey frowned.

"It looks great!"

"It's stupid!" Joey shook his head. "I'm going outside to wait for Dad. See you tomorrow."

After Joe Senior picked up Joey, Sarah drove over to the Boy Scout leader's house. Several dads already waited in line outside the garage for the official weigh-in. They were discussing the tools they'd used, the strategies they'd employed, and the models they'd designed. They were as excited as children—but there wasn't a kid in sight. All of their rocket race cars were as sleek as the ones Sarah and Joey had seen on the Internet.

Once inside the garage, Sarah found herself in a handyman's heaven. The Boy Scout leader laughed when he saw the little iceberg.

"Cute," he said. "And it falls within the weight specifications. You're good to go." He handed it back to her. "See you tomorrow night."

The next evening, the school cafeteria was overflowing with Boy Scouts, dads, friends, and family. Joey was excited, even though he told Sarah that he still thought the iceberg car looked stupid. They'd glued a couple of quarters to the underside of the block, as Sarah had seen one of the fathers do at the weigh-in, hoping to speed up the little car's descent down the long, curved track.

Shaped like a ski ramp, the racetrack was equipped with an electric timer that clocked each race car's time to a hundredth of a second. *Boys and their toys*, thought Sarah.

The races began, and each troop lined up their cars. Joey's troop had a dozen cars, all sleek and shiny; only Joey's was shaped like an iceberg. Only Joey's had plastic penguins on top.

"What kind of car is that?" one of Joey's pals sniggered.

"Is that yours, Joey?" The boys all laughed.

"Go on, honey." Sarah pushed Joey up to the front.

Red-faced, Joey handed his car to the judge, and the judge placed it at the top of the ramp along with the others. He looked at the penguins and winked at Joey.

"Let's wind them up for good luck." He wound up one of the penguins. Even though glued in place, it still wobbled back and forth, as if it were treading water.

The judge laughed, and wound up the rest of them, placing the little car on the starting line just as the race began. Down the ramp flew the little iceberg, its penguins prancing. People pointed and laughed.

"Go, penguins, go!" they shouted. "Go, penguins, go!"

To everyone's enormous surprise—especially Joey's—the little car placed third. Joey got a medal, and Sarah got a big hug. "I can't believe it, Mom!"

Sarah laughed. "Neither can I!"

But the best was yet to come. After all the races were over, the overall prizes were handed out. Grand Prize went to the sleekest, shiniest bullet car there, built by a Boy Scout whose father just happened to be a master carpenter. *Yeah, right*, Sarah thought.

"Next up, the prize for the most original derby car," the Boy Scout leader announced. "Now which car do you think that will be?"

"Penguins! Penguins! Penguins!" the crowd roared.

"That's right! The prize for most original car goes to Joey and his penguins, from Troop 32!"

Joey beamed.

The Boy Scout leader handed him his little silver cup, and asked, "How in the world did you come up with that, Joey?"

Joey looked at Sarah and smiled. "Me and my mom did it. Together."

"That's great! With an imagination like that, you'll go far, Joey! Congratulations!"

On the ride home, Sarah and Joey stopped for ice cream. Over hot-fudge sundaes they replayed every glorious moment of the Pinewood Derby.

"This is the best night ever, Mom!" said Joey, his face streaked with chocolate.

"I'm just glad it worked out," Sarah told Joey.

Joey looked down at his ice cream. "You know, Mom, the car I made with Dad never won anything."

"I see," said Sarah, praying for the good grace not to gloat.

"But our iceberg car totally rocked!"

Sarah laughed. "Come on, time to go."

Back home, Joey washed his face, brushed his teeth, and put on his pajamas. He placed his prize-winning racecar on the bookcase above his bed—a place of honor for the little iceberg car, blessed by the grace of God.

"Time for prayers," Sarah told him.

"Okay," Joey said, and scampered into bed. "God bless my Pinewood Derby car and Mom and Grandpa and Grandpa and Mrs. Harper, my teacher, and Charlie, my best friend, and, uh, amen."

"And your dad," Sarah said gently.

"And Dad."

"Amen."

Joey looked at Sarah. "I can't wait to tell him all about it, Mom. Nathan and Tyler, too."

"I see," said Sarah, and kissed her son good night.

✝ *The Pastor Says* . . .

It's been said that, "Teamwork makes the dream work."

Today, and every day, countless single mothers like Sarah partner with their children to help make their children's dreams come true. These powerful partnerships require patience, wisdom, strength, ingenuity, and lots of bedtime prayers.

Many years ago a wise king—who happened to have 700 wives and 300 concubines—noted that, "Two are better than one." Today, multitudes of mothers—who happen to have zero husbands—embrace this timeless truth as they struggle to forge strong partnerships with their children and maintain confidence that their work will "have a good return." I think it is safe to say that no one understands the power of partnership like a single parent who daily faces the challenges of life without the encouragement, support, and companionship of a loving spouse. And I think it is also safe to say that no one understands the blessings of partnership more than the child of a loving and committed single mother.

Now, in a perfect world, children would not be alone when they wake up in the morning, leave for school, come home from school, do their homework, eat their dinner, and say their prayers before they drift off to sleep. And in a perfect world, mothers would not be left to parent alone, either. But we don't live in a perfect world, so we thank God for mothers like Sarah who teach boys like Joey that teamwork can make Pinewood Derby dreams come true.

—Arron Chambers

Spiritual Lessons in Action

Write the name of someone who has partnered with you to help your dreams come true. Thank God for this person and then thank him or her yourself.

A Third of a Century and Then . . .

By Paul S. Williams

In the same way, the Spirit helps us in our weakness. We do not know what we ought to pray for, but the Spirit himself intercedes for us with groans that words cannot express. And he who searches our hearts knows the mind of the Spirit, because the Spirit intercedes for the saints in accordance with God's will.

—ROMANS 8:26,27

I thought I made my grandfather die.

I had a pet rabbit named Lightning, one of a succession of pet rabbits. My first rabbit was run over by a car. Dad didn't tell me until I was twenty-three years old. He always said, "I dunno, Paul, he just got out of the cage and ran away." Yeah, right, Dad.

We donated another rabbit, Cotton, to the Akron Zoo after it scratched my arm and left a scar I can still see to this day. The zoo had a little rabbit village. Cotton went with the other rabbits into the little rabbit church where they kept the feed. I liked the idea of being fed in church.

Lightning didn't get a chance to chow down on feed at the little rabbit church. One Saturday morning I came downstairs and Dad called me from the basement. "Paul, I have some bad news. Lightning died." There was no apparent cause of death. He just died. But as I walked away from the house toward Pritchard's Drugstore that morning, prepared to drown my grief in a nickel's worth of candy, I worked a ten year old's sad magic.

I knew Papa, my Dad's father, was sick. Dad had told me about the cancer around Christmastime. I vaguely understood the illness was terminal. But I didn't have a very good handle on exactly what that meant. I just knew at some point in the not-too-distant future I would have to experience the same emptiness in the pit of my stomach I had felt five months earlier when Mom's father had died—the same feeling I was having now, at the corner of Roslyn and Maple, as I walked to the drugstore. Moving across the concrete squares, taking care not to step on a single crack, I thought the thought out loud, "If Lightning has to die, then Papa might as well die." There. I said it. I prayed it. And then I stepped on a crack. And just a few days later, Papa died. Just as I had prayed.

I dared not talk to a soul about it. And through all the activity of the funeral I didn't give it much conscious thought. But then we were back in Akron. No Papa. No Lightning. Just the fears of a ten-year-old boy that maybe, just maybe, he had prayed a terrible prayer that an awful God had answered.

I never did talk with anyone about it. I grieved, trudging unknowingly through the cycles of denial, anger, bargaining, depression, and acceptance. Every now and then I remembered what happened at the corner of Roslyn and Maple, but I pushed it aside. I grew up, and the faded and torn memory was relegated to some cobwebbed corner of my heart.

Then came the day I heard someone say the third member of the trinity, the Holy Spirit, prays for us when we cannot pray for ourselves. And I was taken back to the corner of Roslyn and Maple, and my eyes welled with tears. So there had been someone translating for me on that cold April morning. And the words from my mouth had reached the ears of God wet with the tears of the Spirit. "Protect this little one, who knows only of dying, and does not yet understand the other side."

In the mid-nineties we were on vacation, headed to see family in Kentucky and Ohio. We had just driven through the panhandle of West Virginia, and crossed the Ohio River in Wheeling. After getting gas at a station just off the interstate, I looked across the highway to a large cemetery on a hill. Even though I didn't know the location of the cemetery in which my grandfather was buried, I had a sense this serene spot in the gently rolling hills of eastern Ohio was his final resting place. I had only been there once, on an April day in 1961. Yet here it was, the summer of 1994, and I was confident an unhealed memory was nearby.

Over the mild protestations of my family, I headed into the cemetery and drove around until I found a place that felt right. I stopped the car, got out, and started walking past the gravestones. All the markers were flat against the ground. There were no standing marble and granite headstones, just flat stone markers. I thought to myself, "How could I ever find a grave marker in a cemetery like this? You've got to be right on top of the graves before you even see the markers, and then half of those are covered with grass." Still, I began searching. I walked about thirty feet, looked at about ten or fifteen markers, and then my heart caught in my throat. There were my grandparents' graves. I fell to my knees and sobbed. My children retreated to the car. My wife came and touched my shoulders. I pulled weeds away from the marker with my hands. I touched the stone and traced the letters. I had not been to that spot in a third of a century. I had never asked where the grave was. I had not wanted to know.

And now, the stone wet with tears, I finally forgave myself for that child's prayer. And I thanked God that the Spirit speaks for us the words we do not know to speak, and that death is not the final word.

✝ *The Pastor Says* . . .

I struggled for the right words . . . any words.

I recently attended the funeral of a friend, John. He was a strong Christian—a good man who loved his wife and kids divinely. The church was packed. People were willing to stand for over an hour just to be in the same room with others who loved him. It was wonderful. It was terrible.

All death is offensive to God and devastating to humans, but John was only thirty-three, so his death was . . . it just didn't make sense. I love God, I really do, but I'm sad that John's wife and two kids will have to face an empty chair at the dinner table where a loving man once sat.

I couldn't find the words as I stood before John's father. The cancer came out of nowhere. A spot on an ear destroyed a body in only twelve months. John was his only son.

I hate cancer. I love God.

I miss John. I couldn't find the words to speak to John's father.

I prayed but had a hard time finding the words to speak to John's—and my—heavenly Father.

Times like these make me so grateful that the Holy Spirit "helps us in our weakness."

The Christians in Rome were feeling weak and were hurting (Rom. 8:18). They needed to know that they still had hope, so the Apostle Paul writes, "there is now no condemnation for those who are in Christ Jesus" (Rom. 8:1). They also needed to know that Jesus was clinging to them as much as they were clinging to Him, so he reminds them, that nothing "will be able to separate us from the love of God that is in Christ Jesus our Lord" (Rom. 8:39). They needed some assurance that God would not just hear their prayers, but understand them, so Paul assured them that, "The Spirit helps us in our weakness. We do not know what we ought to pray for, but the Spirit himself intercedes for us with groans that words cannot express" (Rom. 8:26).

In the eighth chapter of Romans, we find the Apostle Paul offering words of life, words of hope, and words of victory to people hurt so badly by life that all they could do was "groan." Paul writes, "We know that the whole creation has been groaning as in the pains of childbirth right up to the present time. Not only so, but we ourselves, who have the first fruits of the Spirit, groan inwardly as we wait eagerly for our adoption as sons, the redemption of our bodies" (Rom. 8:22, 23).

It's been my experience that groaning hinders communication. Ever been punched in the gut? Ever been the victim of a cheap shot? Ever felt a pain that doubled you over? Hard to speak when you're in pain, isn't it?

When life punches you in the gut, when life takes a cheap shot, when life causes a pain in your soul that doubles you over, and it's hard to speak to God, or find strength in the confidence that in our weakness the Holy Spirit stands beside us in God's presence, with a hand on our shoulder, and says, "Here's what he's trying to say." God, through the work of the Holy Spirit, sees what we can't show and hears what we can't say.

I finally thought of what I wanted to say to God about John and his family: "Lord, I love you. I trust you. Please help John's family during this time of great pain. Amen.

"Lord, I also want to pray for the person who is reading these words right now. This person and I are sharing this path with you because we trust you and want to be where you are and follow you to where you are going. Lord, we both know that this journey will lead us through times of joy and times of suffering. Lord, in those times when grief makes the right words hard to find, I pray that your Holy Spirit will say what my friend can't say. Amen."

—Arron Chambers

Spiritual Lessons in Action

Contact someone who is grieving the loss of a loved one.
Share with that person what Paul says in
Romans 8:26,27 and then pray with him or her.

Begonia Roots

By Laurie Alice Eakes

That same day Jesus went out of the house and sat by the lake. Such large crowds gathered around him that he got into a boat and sat in it, while all the people stood on the shore. Then he told them many things in parables, saying: "A farmer went out to sow his seed. As he was scattering the seed, some fell along the path, and the birds came and ate it up. Some fell on rocky places, where it did not have much soil. It sprang up quickly, because the soil was shallow. But when the sun came up, the plants were scorched, and they withered because they had no root. Other seed fell among thorns, which grew up and choked the plants. Still other seed fell on good soil, where it produced a crop—a hundred, sixty or thirty times what was sown. He who has ears, let him hear."

—MATTHEW 13:1–9

Thirty-five boxes of books. Check. Five boxes of dishes and other fragile items. Check. Two oversize crates of linens. Check. The list scrolled on to reach seventy containers altogether. Not much stuff, a mover had claimed during the last relocation. Maybe not for a professional mover. But this time, friends had offered to haul our worldly goods the eighteen miles from one Washington, DC suburb to another.

The foothill of boxes looked like Everest to me. This was the eleventh city I was moving to in twenty-five years, and I had also moved within those cities. I felt like a plant, a begonia, easily uprooted from its shallow depth, and sure to wither if improperly replanted.

My plants were always improperly planted. I could kill mint, let alone a more finicky begonia. What part of my life would die in this move?

One moving truck parked. Check. Three friends arrived, and one more was on the way. Check. Cat in her crate, and dogs leashed. Check.

"What do you want to put in the attic?" Bonnie yelled. A Coast Guard Academy graduate, she sounded as though she could have been heard down the decks of an eighteenth-century frigate, as she referred to the shelf above the truck cab.

"We'll load boxes there first," I answered. That was my first mistake of the day.

Everyone started carrying boxes downstairs. Piles of book crates transferred to a wall inside the truck.

"Stop," I shouted. I didn't have Bonnie's air of command, and no one listened to me.

The boxes piled up in and outside the truck until Eric, my husband's coworker, declared, "We can't get the big furniture in there."

"But we have to." My heart began to race, breath catching in my throat. *I will not have a panic attack this early in the day.*

I was about to, though, for we only had a two-hour window during which we were allowed to use the loading dock and freight elevator in our new apartment building. In no way could we unload the truck, return to the apartment we were moving out of, load the rest of the furniture, then return with the second haul and ferry it up to the seventh floor in two hours. We had to turn the truck in by 9:00 the following morning, and we couldn't get another move-in time that early.

To keep myself calm, I returned upstairs to the apartment and sat in a desk chair. That was my second mistake of the day. Everyone thought I was sitting by, doing nothing. No, I wasn't hauling boxes and furniture, but I was doing something—regrouping, wondering why everything that seemed to have gone well thus far was suddenly falling apart. Hadn't I prayed diligently for deliverance from calamity, as I did with every move?

Every move . . . every escape from one living situation that had become intolerable for one reason or another. What was wrong with me that I could never settle anywhere long enough to put down roots and blossom? I was more like that rolling stone that gathers no moss, impossible that I could bear any fruit.

With nothing to do but persevere, I staggered to my feet and began directing traffic in a more efficient way. We would simply have to talk the building manager into allowing us extra time with the loading dock. I'd send in my husband, Gene, with his considerable charm. We were making this move for him, weren't we? I was giving up more than he was—my home office; my desk; one of my bookcases, a big one I'd put together myself. But he needed a desk for law school, and I, with only one book contract under my belt, was supposed to be able to work anywhere.

"Location. Location. Location," I chanted as I ran around the flat looking for those odds and ends that had gotten left behind. I'd always moved for location. The grass was always greener over the next state line, city limits, housing development. Would this new location prove green, gray, or the black depression I felt creeping toward me?

Maybe the last feeling was just a headache coming on. I'd begun to lift boxes far heavier than I was supposed to. I carried furniture and advised on positioning inside the truck, since I was the one with experience moving. I began to hate the sound of my own name with everyone yelling, "Laurie, what do you want me to do with . . . ?"

"Just throw it in the box," I snapped at Bonnie in regard to some small items she'd found behind a printer stand. She did—literally.

I raised my eyebrows. "Was that necessary?"

"Is your behavior necessary?" Gene asked.

"What have I done wrong?" The question was sincere, but the answer was obvious—everything.

"These people are giving up their Saturday to help you," my husband continued. "The least you can do is be nice to them."

"They're not here to help me." Tears pricked my eyes. "They're your friends."

Resentment mingling with self-pity oozed from every pore. I'd lived in Northern Virginia for over two-and-a-half years, and at that moment, I felt as though I didn't have a single friend close at hand. My friends lived in Pittsburgh, last I knew; in Iowa, last I knew; in Kentucky, Tennessee, Texas, New Jersey, and Illinois, last I knew. I never put down roots deep enough in one place for relationships to grow, either, let alone flourish enough to withstand time and distance. Most of my contact with humans, other than casual acquaintances at work, occurred through e-mail and discussion boards, where I could never get close to anyone.

"I'm tired of this," my husband said.

"So am I," I responded.

We didn't say what "this" was, but we both knew—disconnectedness. Gene's friends from work didn't even know he was going to law school. Until he finished negotiations with his company over whether or not he would continue to work for them and in what capacity, management didn't want him to say anything. That distanced him from his friends. Our work schedules had isolated us. We didn't even know the names of the neighbors in the apartment complex where we'd lived for two-and-a-half years. Instead of drawing us closer together, the strain was tugging us apart from one another, too. I felt as though God had ignored my prayers for the day to go smoothly.

Then the miracle happened. A bit over halfway through our two hours of loading-dock time, another truck pulled up. An irate gentleman insisted that he had the time scheduled and we needed to get out of there. I was furious. We'd had that slot scheduled for two weeks. The man was lying, I was sure.

Gene saw the situation for what it was—the break we needed. My husband persuaded the front desk clerk on duty to reopen the loading dock later that night. This gave us the time we needed to return to our apartment, collect the last of our furniture, and return to the building.

Starving, we went to the local IHOP two blocks away and ate. Then, when everyone else went home, Gene and I tumbled into bed. The next morning, I woke, expecting the same despair I'd felt the day before. None of the furniture was where I wanted it. I had seventy boxes to move around in order to place furniture properly before I could begin unpacking. Yet I stood on the sun porch with the vista of the city surrounding me, and thought what a lovely room it would make for plants, with its floor-to-ceiling windows on three sides.

I, the person who couldn't put down roots, was thinking of procuring houseplants? I'd given up on those years ago. Yet I kept thinking about a housewarming present someone had given me many years ago—a begonia. I'd thought them the most beautiful flowers I'd ever seen. They died because I didn't plant them properly. They have shallow roots, are easily transferred to pots for indoors during the winter, and will bloom and bloom and bloom if properly cared for. Although I'd failed with those begonias, I never forgot how much they pleased me while they lasted. Now I realized that I could try again with greater knowledge of how to raise a begonia and make it flourish.

Like that begonia, I, too, grew with shallow roots, easily transplanted to where I needed to live, not simply to survive, but to flourish, grow, and benefit those around me. With the right attitude, I could look at each move not as running away, but running toward my next opportunity to grow and benefit those around me.

✝ *The Pastor Says . . .*

I want to share a parable with you. I once heard a teacher say that parables are traps.

On one occasion, Jesus told a story about a farmer, seeds, and a dream. All farmers dream of a bountiful harvest, and all bountiful harvests begin with seeds. Farmers depend on seeds to do what they cannot do on their own. Jesus described how the farmer scattered his seed along a path. Some of the seed fell on the path where it could not take root, so it was immediately devoured by hungry birds. Some fell on rocky soil that prevented the growth of deep roots. The seed grew into plants, but the roots were shallow, so the plants died when the sun came up. Some seed fell among thorns—and took root—but soon the thorns won, choking the life out of the plants before they could produce. Some seed fell on good soil, where it produced a ginormous (to borrow a word from my daughter) crop. The trap is set.

The disciples of Jesus want to know what this means, so he tells them. The seed is the message about the kingdom of God. The birds who snatch the seed before it takes root represent the work of the Devil. The rocky soil is the person who comes to Christ only to later fall away from faith when life gets difficult. The thorny soil is the person who allows the worries of this world to choke the life out of his or her faith. The good soil is the person who hears what Jesus has to say, understands it, believes it, and lives it.

The trap springs!

I can almost see the awareness come across the Disciples' faces as they realize that Jesus has a dream. Again, all farmers dream of a bountiful harvest, and all bountiful harvests begin with seeds. He's the farmer and we are the soil and He wants, He expects his followers to produce.

God expects us to share His love with His people.

God expects us to serve one another.

God expects us to share hope with hopeless people.

God expects us to help the hurting.

God expects us to be a companion to the lonely.
And God expects begonias to bloom.

—Arron Chambers

Spiritual Lessons in Action

Stop by a local nursery and buy a pack of seeds.
On the packet of seeds I want you to write a dream
you'd like to accomplish in the next year. Keep the
packet in your wallet, or purse, as a reminder of
your dream and of God's dream for your life.

Beneath the Ice

By Susan Page Davis

D o not let your hearts be troubled.
Trust in God; trust also in me. In my
Father's house are many rooms; if it
were not so, I would have told you. I am going
there to prepare a place for you. And if I go and
prepare a place for you, I will come back and
take you to be with me that you also may be
where I am."

—JOHN 14:1–3

Faye waddled out onto the ice in her cumber-
some wool snowsuit. She and her friend Mim,
ages five and six, didn't have ice skates, so they
slid along the smooth, slippery surface in their
boots while the older children and teenagers
laced up their skates.

Faye's big brother, Ken, sped out onto the
vast smoothness with the other teens. They
laughed and called to each other, skating far
out on the mile-wide lake, leaving the younger
children near shore.

Mim's older sister, Pam, and her brother, Gil, sat on their mittens while pulling on their skates. Once he was laced up, Gil glided onto the ice with several friends. A short distance from shore, the ice had heaved and cracked, forming a pressure ridge a couple of feet high. Pam and the boys climbed carefully over it.

Faye and Mim joined them. They ran a few steps, then slid. Faye hoped she could get skates for Christmas next year, so she could learn to skate like the big kids.

It was bitterly cold. She wished her snowsuit had a hood, like the other kids' did. Instead, her fiery red hair was hidden under a brown wool hat with flaps that covered her ears and that tied beneath her chin. The hat matched her brown wool snowsuit. She hated it. The suit was snug, itchy, and uncomfortable, but her mother insisted on wool because of Faye's previous bouts with tonsillitis. She had to keep warm in the Maine winters.

The only colorful parts of her costume were the blue scarf and mittens her Nana had knit for her. Icy wind pulled at the ends of the scarf, but the wool suit kept her from shivering.

Gil circled and skimmed back toward them with long, smooth strokes. He was ten, and protective of his younger sisters.

"You girls keep away from that hole over there," he warned. Mim and Faye looked where he pointed. Behind an inviting slope of the ice ridge, a small gap of open water showed.

The girls played a few yards offshore while Gil and the other boys skated. Faye, Mim, and eight-year-old Pam chased each other and slid, shouting with glee. Faye's feet went out from under her, and she plopped down on her seat, but the thick snowsuit protected her.

Mim climbed the highest ridge of ice. Though only three feet tall, the slope was so slick she had to crawl up, reaching for the top and pulling herself up. She sat on the crest for a moment.

"Look out!" Mim pushed off and slid down the hill toward Faye, almost bowling her over. Faye dodged out of the way too quickly, and thudded down on her seat again. Soon the two littlest girls, with Pam, were taking turns crawling up the slope and sliding down.

Faye approached the ridge with determination. Her boots and snowsuit gave her a little traction, but it was still hard to gain the top without sliding backward. She stretched for the summit, curling her hands over the edge of the broken ice. Clutching it through her mittens, she hauled herself up. When her face was even with her hands, she looked over the edge. A yard below her, she saw the hole in the ice.

The water was beginning to freeze over, closing the hole, but it was still open in the middle. The sheet of ice supporting them must be more than a foot thick, Faye thought. Sometimes her father made holes in the ice to fish through. She wondered if there were fish down there in the dark water. She pulled herself higher to get a better look at the hole, and suddenly she was falling down the back of the ridge.

Her hands hit the hole first, then her head. As the rest of her body followed, she felt suddenly heavy. Her wool snowsuit soaked up water, pulling her down.

Lower and lower she went, falling in slow motion. She couldn't stop.

Faye opened her eyes and blinked. It was dark. Her hands touched the bottom of the lake. In summer, when she swam there, her father kept her in the shallows. She couldn't really swim yet, but she had learned to stand up if she needed a breath. Now she pushed against the squishy bottom and turned upward, shoving hard with her boots.

Far above, she saw dim light, diffused through the ice, and she wasn't afraid. *I'm going up*, she thought.

In one small spot over her head, a brighter, clearer light shone. *That's the hole*, she told herself.

She tried to move her arms, but the heavy snowsuit fought her movements. She got her hands to her chest and began scooping with them in the dog-paddle motion she had learned last summer.

Far away, she heard voices. "Faye fell in! Faye fell in!"

Staring up at the hole, she saw blobs that must be faces. She pulled harder with her hands, struggling against the water.

She was near the hole now. For an instant, she looked off underneath the ice sheet, and her heart raced with excitement, not fear. It just goes on forever! She stared for a long moment, wondering where the fish were. They must be out there, somewhere, in the endless lake. She wished she could see them!

She looked up again, and the hole was right above her. With one last, huge push, she thrust her hands upward. Immediately, strong fingers clutched her wrists. She was lifted higher, until she flopped out of the hole and lay on top of the ice, gasping. Only then did she realize she had been holding her breath—how long? It seemed like ages. And she was achingly cold. The sensation struck her suddenly. All over, it felt like knives were scraping her skin.

Gil pulled her away from the hole. "Are you all right?" He tried to let go of her, but their wet mittens were already freezing together, and he had to peel his away from hers.

"Faye!" Mim's face was almost against hers as her anxious little friend peered at her. "Are you alive?"

"I think so." Her teeth began to chatter. She was so cold.

"What happened?" She looked up as the shout came and saw her brother skating swiftly toward her.

"Faye fell through the ice," Gil told him.

"You'd better go home," Ken said, looking her over.

Faye rolled over and pushed up onto her knees. Pam reached out to help her rise.

"Are you sure you're okay?" Gil asked.

Faye couldn't stop shivering.

"Go home as fast as you can," Ken said. "Mim, can you go with her?"

Mim nodded, her blue eyes huge in her pale face.

Gil helped the little girls up the path to the road. "You'll be all right," he assured them. "Just go straight to Faye's house."

Faye trudged along beside her friend. She had never been so cold. The wind cut into her now, and strands of hair were freezing on her forehead. Her feet were going numb.

"You've got icicles on your eyelashes," Mim said in awe.

It hurt to breathe in the biting cold air. Faye clamped her lips shut and kept walking. Her home was half a mile from the lake, and it usually didn't seem far.

"You can make it," Mim said, as if reading her thoughts. There was fear in Mim's eyes, and a shiver of anxiety went through Faye's mind. *What if I freeze to death?*

Her mittens were so hard she couldn't make a fist, and her clothes stiffened as she walked. Each step was harder than the one before.

"Come on," Mim said urgently.

"Who's that?" Faye gasped, and Mim looked ahead at the figure approaching.

"It's Pat."

Pat was the oldest of Mim's siblings. She came toward them, swinging her skates by the laces. As she came closer, she opened her mouth and stared at Faye. "What happened to you? You look like a giant icicle!"

"Faye fell through the ice," Mim squeaked, her voice cracking. "Gil pulled her out."

"We've got to get you home!" Pat took Faye's hand and hustled her toward home. "I can't believe those boys let you walk home like this! They should have carried you! Come on! We're almost there."

Faye focused on putting one numb foot ahead of the other. They reached the driveway, and Mim ran ahead and pounded on the door.

Suddenly Faye was in her father's arms. Her mother unbuttoned her snowsuit and lifted the frozen cap gently from her head. Someone wrapped a blanket around her.

"Run some hot water in the bathtub," she heard her mother say, and she wondered if she would ever be warm again. Her father smelled of pipe tobacco and cedar shavings. She snuggled down against his cozy flannel shirt and closed her eyes.

"Daddy," she said, "Can I learn to swim?"

✝ *The Pastor Says* . . .

It's amazing, in life, how happiness can turn to heartache in an instant. In seconds, fun can turn to fear, joy can turn to grief, and laughter can turn to crying.

We are familiar with the stories: Teens driving home after a carefree evening at prom lose control of the car and end up broken, bleeding, and fighting for their lives on the side of a lonely road.

A fire bursts through a crowded bar. A plane full of vacationers crashes in the mountains. One minute you can be laughing with your friends, playing on the ice, and the next minute you—like Faye—can be fighting for your life, desperate for hope, trying to swim.

The Disciples' world was about to change. They didn't know it, but Jesus did. The peace they felt dining with Jesus in the upstairs room would turn to fear in just a few hours as their host would be arrested in a local olive grove. In the next twenty-four hours they were going to see their master, their leader, their friend arrested, mocked, executed, and buried. Life is like that sometimes.

Knowing this, Jesus says exactly what he knows his disciples need to know before they know they need to know it. "Do not let your hearts be troubled. Trust in God; trust also in me." He is saying it now—at the eleventh hour—because he wants these words to still be ringing in their ears when their world is turned upside down. Jesus wants his disciples to have hope and to know that when they fall through the ice, he is not going to let them drown. When they are helpless, they will not be hopeless. When their world turns dark and cold and the light above seems a million miles away, He wants them to swim and keep swimming. He says, "If I go and prepare a place for you, I will come back and take you to be with me that you also may be where I am." You and I must remember that with Jesus we have a Savior—someone who will always come back for us, someone who will always reach down into the darkness to pull us to the light, and someone who promises to take us to our safe, beautiful, and eternal home, where we'll never be cold again. Jesus won't leave us beneath the ice. He will rescue us. We just have to keep swimming.

—Arron Chambers

Spiritual Lessons in Action

List two of the biggest challenges you are facing today. Now, after each challenge, list a promise from God's Word that assures you that you will overcome that specific challenge. After you are finished, write "Keep swimming!" across the top of the list.

What Do You Do with All That Money?

By Bob Russell

Now a man came up to Jesus and asked, "Teacher, what good thing must I do to get eternal life?"

"Why do you ask me about what is good?" Jesus replied. "There is only One who is good. If you want to enter life, obey the commandments."

"Which ones?" the man inquired.

Jesus replied, "'Do not murder, do not commit adultery, do not steal, do not give false testimony, honor your father and mother,' and 'love your neighbor as yourself.'"

"All these I have kept," the young man said. "What do I still lack?"

Jesus answered, "If you want to be perfect, go, sell your possessions and give to the poor, and you will have treasure in heaven. Then come, follow me."

When the young man heard this, he went away sad, because he had great wealth.

Then Jesus said to his disciples, "I tell you the truth, it is hard for a rich man to enter the kingdom of heaven. Again I tell you, it is easier for a camel to go through the eye of a needle than for a rich man to enter the kingdom of God."

—MATTHEW 19:16—24

A year ago I met a multimillionaire named Paul J. Meyer. Many call him the most generous man alive. When Paul was sixteen years old his strict, uncompromising father kicked him out of the house and told him not to come back. He lived as a homeless young man, and for several months slept in a tent.

But Paul was determined to make the most of his life, and soon he had a job with an insurance company collecting monthly payments. That wasn't a very glamorous job, but it was a job. He was so faithful in his assigned task that eventually he was given an opportunity to sell insurance.

By the time he was thirty years old, the ambitious, determined Paul J. Meyer became the National Salesman of the Year for his company. He then began teaching sales seminars and has since written numerous training courses and invested wisely, making millions.

But years ago the Lord touched his heart, and Paul became convinced that there was something better to do with his money than just accumulate more and more. He began giving huge amounts away. He discovered that it was indeed "more blessed to give than to receive." He loved the joy and sense of satisfaction he got from helping others.

Today Paul J. Meyer is in his seventies and gives away more than 90 percent of what he earns. He's incredibly generous with worthy causes and has put more than 500 kids through college.

I serve on the board of a national ministry with Paul J. Meyer, but I hadn't met him personally until last year when, during a participation activity, I found myself sitting between him and his lawyer/financial advisor. There were just three of us at the table for the next forty-five minutes.

When I began probing a little about his generosity, his financial advisor laughingly said, "It's my job to make sure that Paul doesn't give his money away faster than we take it in!" He said that several years ago the two of them took a weeklong drive across the Midwest, and Paul passed his business card out to ten different young people he'd just met saying, "Call this number, and I'll help put you through college." But nine of the ten never called because they didn't believe it was for real.

The accountant said, "We were stopped at a highway construction site and Meyer was intrigued with a young girl dressed in blue jeans, wearing a helmet, holding a stop sign. He leaned out the window and struck up a conversation with her.

"Why are you working on construction?"

She said, "I'm working my way through college."

He asked, "Can't your parents help you?"

She answered, "No, they're not in a position to help right now."

He asked, "What do you want to be?"

"My dream is to become a nurse someday," she replied.

Paul J. Meyer gave her his card and said, "Young lady, I'm in the business of making dreams come true. Next week you call this number and I'll see that you have the money to go to college."

The next week the financial advisor got a phone call and the girl on the other end of the line said, "Last week some little old man said he'd help pay my way through college if I called this number. Is that true?"

He happily replied, "Yes, ma'am, it is."

As they told that story the faces of both lit up as they excitedly described how this young woman is now a nurse in a Midwestern hospital because they had the resources to share with her.

Wouldn't that be fun? Wouldn't you love to have millions to give away to those in need? The thought occurred to me that maybe that's why Paul J. Meyer has it to give away. The Bible says, "Give, and it will be given to you. A good measure, pressed down, shaken together and running over, will be poured into your lap. For with the measure you use, it will be measured to you" (Luke 6:38 NIV). But the real test is not what you'd do if you were a multimillion-aire, but what you are doing with what you have right now. One poet quipped, "It's not what you'd do with a million if riches should ever be your lot, but what you're doing right now with the dollar and a quarter you've got."

† *The Pastor Says* . . .

Once a good man came to Jesus with a difficult question: "What good thing must I do to get eternal life?" This man was rich, young, and probably a leader in a local synagogue. He was a believer in God—keeping all of the commandments of God—but he was yet to become a follower. Believing in and following are two very different things.

This young wealthy man had an impressive temporal life full of great wealth, but he wanted even more. He wanted eternal life, too. He wasn't asking too much—he just wanted one simple thing he could do to earn eternal life!

Isn't that how we are? We want a magic pill that will allow us to lose in one week the weight we spent thirty years accumulating. We want one-minute solutions to lifelong problems.

This man wanted easy eternal life. Anyone who knows the heart of God knows that it is absurd to think that we can do anything to earn eternal life, but Jesus played along, answering his "simple" request with a "simple" answer: "Obey the commandments."

To which the rich young leader answered what Jesus knew he would answer: "I've kept all of these, what do I still lack?"

To which Jesus answered: "If you want to be perfect, go, sell your possessions and give to the poor, and you will have treasure in heaven. Then come, follow me."

Greed is a powerful force and hard to walk away from, but there is a force much more powerful than greed and that force is generosity.

Paul J. Meyer knows the power of generosity. He gave in to the power of giving, and now he can't—he won't—walk away. When it appears that all everybody wants is to have more, all Paul wants is to give more. He can't give his money away fast enough. Generosity has consumed him. He chose Jesus and walks behind Him with a smile on his face.

Jesus knows the power of generosity. Jesus is the embodiment of generosity. In his life he gave healing to hurting people, time to lonely people, wisdom to seekers, food to the hungry, sight to the blind, fish to the hungry, comfort to the inconsolable, hope to the hopeless, purpose to the lost, and mercy to the sinners. Then, in the greatest act of generosity, in His death He gave life to the dead. His generosity consumed Him, yet He still keeps on giving. That's the power of generosity.

Every day, we need to decide what we are going to do. Will we give in to the power of generosity, or the power of greed?

Will we walk with Jesus smiling, or will we walk away—and alone—sad?

—Arron Chambers

Spiritual Lessons in Action

Do something generous for a stranger today. Pick up the lunch tab for the older couple in the corner booth. Pay for the groceries of the young mother who is checking out just ahead of you. Buy a bag of groceries for a needy college kid. Enjoy giving in to the power of giving.

Ducks on a Pond

By Kenneth R. Funk

B e very careful, then, how you live—not as unwise but as wise, making the most of every opportunity, because the days are evil.

—EPHESIANS 5:15,16

"Ducks on a pond," he used to say. I lost my dad a couple of years ago to a heart attack. I never got to tell him so many things I wanted to tell him because he was taken so quickly. I often think of him, the impact he has had on my life, and the impact that he has made on my kids' lives and on the lives of my staff at work, through me. He was a man of character, commitment, integrity, and passion, who approached life with a tremendous competitive spirit. Like most fathers, he worked a full-time job, but what made him different was that in addition to having a second job to help the family make ends meet, he never ever passed up an opportunity to be involved in my life, or my brother's life, or my sister's life.

When I was eight years old in the summer of 1973, I remember that I got to play "big kid" baseball for the first time. I had played T-ball and peewee ball, but this was the "big time." Where I grew up it was *the* thing to do—a rite of passage. It was a typical summer in west central Oklahoma. The oppressive heat made even the locusts cry for relief, and the incessant wind seemed to push every cloud out of the sky. The combination of the wind and the heat made it feel like a blast furnace outside—and we were always outside.

In the days before video games, and with only three channels on the TV, there was no reason to be inside. Rain or shine, we were at the ball field. In the distance was the constant rumbling of oil derricks and combines threshing wheat. The smell of pine tar, freshly scraped infield dirt, and tattered leather from our baseball mitts permeated the air. There was always the anticipation of the opportunity. It's a summer I will never forget.

My dad was our coach. His competitiveness and desire to win were matched only by his patience and his desire to teach. He took his two-week vacation that year and devoted nearly every second of it to us. We spent hours and hours working on how to play the game. No detail was too small. No stone was left unturned. Much to our mothers' dismay, we would come home every day covered head to toe with sweat, dirt, grass stains, and the occasional battle scar from meeting the metal spikes from our teammates' shoes. I recollect swinging my Mickey Mantle Louisville Slugger bat until there were blisters on my hands. There was nothing we would have rather been doing. We were being prepared for something. It wasn't until much later in my life that I figured out what.

In "eight-year-old time" it seemed like we practiced forever before the first game that year, but the reality was that it was probably only a couple of weeks. During games that summer, each time one of the boys would walk to home plate to bat with base runners on second or third base, or both, my dad would shout out, "Ducks on a pond!" I could only guess that he had heard it when he was a boy playing baseball, or that it had something to do with hunting (which was a popular pastime when there wasn't baseball to be played). I wasn't sure of the origin of the expression, though I remember thinking, even as a kid, what an odd thing it was to say on a baseball field.

Nevertheless, I understood what he meant. He meant that if we got a hit in that situation, we would score and most likely win the game. He meant that if we did what we were taught in all those hours of practice, we would succeed. It wasn't until much later in my life that I realized he was focused on a much bigger picture.

Well, our Hillcrest Hawks baseball team went undefeated that year. Thirteen wins without a loss. No other team really even came close to beating us. We had prepared to do a job, and we got it done. Yes, there were times when some of us had mental lapses and made mistakes that cost the team, or times when we failed to capitalize on an opportunity. After all, we were eight years old. But with all the training and preparation and encouragement and forgiveness, we were equipped to succeed in the long term, in spite of any temporary setbacks.

I heard that simple phrase "Ducks on a pond" throughout the time I played baseball, either from the dugout when I was younger, or from the cheering section as I grew older and after my dad had long since hung up his coaching whistle. I continued to hear that expression in my head like a broken record when opportunities presented themselves throughout my childhood, my adolescence, and into my college years. What I didn't realize was that others had heard it also.

In the days following my father's funeral as my mother, brother, sister, and I grieved and looked at cards, letters, and the guest register from the funeral home, we more than once read the phrase, "Ducks on a pond. Thanks, Paul!"—written by kids who played on his team over thirty years earlier. The boys, with whom I spent most every waking hour of that summer long ago, had grown into men now and had come back from all over the country remembering that same phrase that my dad had spoken so often.

It was apparent that my dad had left a legacy—not just the legacy of a peculiar motivational baseball phrase—but the legacy of young boys who had grown into men and who understood the importance of recognizing and capitalizing on opportunities.

As providence would have it, I am now coaching baseball for my eight-year-old son's team. At a game last spring, as he came to the home plate to hit, something mysterious happened. Out of my mouth came the words that my dad used so often in that summer of 1973. "Ducks on a pond!" I yelled. Of course I got a few odd looks. But I also got a look from my son. He seemed to understand what I meant.

It was then and only then that I fully realized what that simple, peculiar phrase had meant. My dad was not just preparing me to succeed in baseball. He was preparing me to succeed in life. He was teaching me to train and prepare to do my best to succeed at any endeavor in which I engaged. He was teaching me to be a leader—a leader by example. We were all better for having heard that expression, though none of us realized it at the time.

Preparing my team, or my family, or my church, or my staff to succeed is as critical to me now as it was to my father then. Who knows where I would be, or where the other kids on that team would be, if not for the lessons we were taught in the summer of 1973?

I have lost track of every one of those boys now, having moved away from my hometown many years ago. I look at the "1973 Undefeated OK Kids City Championship" picture from time to time when I am looking through old pictures and clippings. Every time I see it, I am convinced that each one of those boys is better for having been taught those valuable life lessons during that hot Oklahoma summer.

I am certain that each of them has become better than he would have otherwise been as a result of what we learned that year. I know I am a better leader because of it. And just as it was when I was a kid playing ball, I am going to make mistakes and fail to seize a few opportunities, but with diligence and preparation and encouragement and accountability and forgiveness, the chances are good that I can be successful.

Dad was right: "Ducks on a pond!"

✝ *The Pastor Says* . . .

Today has 1,440 minutes. Every year has 525,600. The typical life has 39,420,000.

Every minute of every day of every year of every typical life is an opportunity. Every opportunity is a chance to grow into more, or shrink into less. Some opportunities are divine and some are not.

Knowing not every opportunity is a good opportunity, in Ephesians Paul warns, "Be very careful, then, how you live—

not as unwise but as wise, making the most of every opportunity, because the days are evil" (Ephesians 5:15,16).

We must make good choices. Seek the Lord. Seek the lost. Redeem the times. And we must be careful.

Paul's correct, "The days are evil" (Ephesians 5:16) and the nights will, in the future, never end in the place prepared for those who choose to embrace evil opportunities and reject divine ones. Paul is writing to Christians who, in their former reality outside of Christ, were "darkness" (Eph. 5:8). Notice, Paul doesn't say they lived in darkness; he says that they "*were once darkness*" (emphasis mine). Choosing to embrace opportunities for evil transforms us from light into darkness incarnate. Opportunities for evil are as equally abundant as opportunities for good, but those who choose to do good are few. Affirming this, Jesus said, "Wide is the gate and broad is the road that leads to destruction, and many enter through it. But small is the gate and narrow the road that leads to life, and only a few find it" (Mt. 7:13, 14).

Quoting the Prophet Isaiah, Paul writes, "Wake up, O sleeper, rise from the dead, and Christ will shine on you" (Eph. 5:14). Paul wants these Christians to wake up to the reality that the ducks are on the pond! They are standing at the plate and there are runners in scoring position. We are standing at the plate.

It's been said that, "Opportunity only knocks once." This is an idiom that means that you only get one chance to achieve what you really want to do. I think only idiots believe this idiom.

I think God immerses us in opportunities. I think He surrounds us with opportunities. I think He daily sends opportunities to our door—occasionally, we hear the knock; rarely, we open the door; and almost never do we recognize opportunity for who He really is.

We say things like: "You must have the wrong house," "I'm not going to accept that—it costs too much," "You want the guy next door," "I'm not ready. Can you come back later?" or "That's too nice. That can't be for me. You must be looking for the person down the street." I don't think the problem is a lack of opportunity, but the inability to recognize opportunity when it's standing on your front porch.

That's why coaches yell things like, "Ducks on a pond!"

Coach Funk yelled this to his baseball team to help them recognize an opportunity. He wanted them to see it so they could seize it. He knew that they needed help to recognize that this was not just another play, but an opportunity to win.

This is what the Apostle Paul is doing in Ephesians 5:14–16. It's as if he's saying, "Be very careful, then, how you live—not as unwise but as wise, because the ducks are on the pond!"

What about you? Can you recognize opportunity when it's knocking on your door? What do you see when your wife is on the front porch, and she's asking you to come home early from work so you can talk? What do you see when your son is on the front porch asking you to play catch after dinner? What do you see when a coworker is on the front porch, admitting trouble in his marriage and asking you if you have time to talk? What do you see when that homeless guy is on your front porch—again—asking if there's anything that you can possibly do to help?

Looks to me like the ducks are on the pond. So, you better not strike out.

—Arron Chambers

Spiritual Lessons in Action

Get your planner, organizer, or calendar, and open it up to today and pray this prayer: "Lord, I don't want to miss any opportunity today. I want to be a blessing to someone. Please give me the discernment and the courage to do exactly what you want me to do today. Amen." Now, plan your day accordingly, leaving room for a few divine appointments.

The Cave

By Timothy W. Jones

S o I have come down to rescue them from the hand of the Egyptians and to bring them up out of that land into a good and spacious land, a land flowing with milk and honey—the home of the Canaanites, Hittites, Amorites, Perizzites, Hivites, and Jebusites. And now the cry of the Israelites has reached me, and I have seen the way the Egyptians are oppressing them. So now, go. I am sending you to Pharaoh to bring my people the Israelites out of Egypt.

—EXODUS 3:8–10

We should all appreciate the artists of this world. And we should never go cave exploring with them.

We were all at a teen convention in eastern Kentucky, and my friends—Dave and Mike—and I (all three artists) had promised a group of teens from Florida that we would take them caving. Hoping for the genuine Appalachian thrill of crawling on bellies in a subterranean labyrinth, I was disappointed to find the local cave merely a tunnel—just one boring fifteen-minute walk in ankle-deep water. Other youth groups had gone caving that day as well, and I was in the midst of apologizing for the ho-hum nature of this cave, when I overheard some guy passing us in the dark tunnel. With a strong Michigan accent, he was singing the praises of some exhilarating cave experience he'd had.

"It obviously wasn't this cave," I wisecracked, and we shined our flashlights at each other.

"Yeah, actually it was," he answered. He told us his name was Ike and that there was a lesser-known passageway in the cave that was challenging and offered a big payoff. He pointed his flashlight up at the roof of the cave. "You end up poking your head out of that hole way up there (about thirty feet up), and you can peer down on everyone going through the cave. And there's a ledge slightly below the opening that someone can sit on." This last sentence would alter my destiny forever.

He took us back toward the entrance and showed us the slick log that you had to prop up against the rock wall. After climbing that, you'd see a small opening. You'd wriggle through that for a while, reach a place that went straight up (you'd have to wedge your elbows just right to ascend), then you'd go up a long slope, with only about a two-foot ceiling, then . . . the top of the cave.

Perhaps it was my crazed grin that alarmed them, but several of the kids decided they'd had their fill of caving and told us they'd wait outside. So Dave and Mike and I led these five hardy adventurers on the "challenger trail": the log, the straight-up elbow wedge, the long slope, the claustrophobia, the muck—I was in cave heaven.

Just when we thought we'd surely taken a wrong turn, we found it: an opening wide enough for two or three people to poke their heads out. We all took turns looking down, giggling, and freaking out the cavers below by yelling things like "You have angered the mountain god!" After about five minutes of this, the novelty wore off, and—I suppose—our adventure would have ended there, had I not shined my flashlight out the opening and exclaimed, "Hey there's that ledge that Ike said you could sit on!" Here's where our party divided: Mike and the teens remembered Ike saying, "Someone could sit on the ledge" while Dave and I recalled it as "People do sit on it."

After some debate on that point, Mike said he'd take the Floridians back the way they came, and if Dave and I wanted to put ourselves in harm's way, good luck. "Pansies!" Dave and I called after them as they slid down the passageway.

Something should have alerted me that day: Dave was the only one agreeing with me. My friend Dave is a big galoot. (He's like that big dog that slips into your small house, whereupon your mother chases him out with a broom, his floppy tail knocking down knick-knacks along the way.) He will say "Yes!" to any suggestion that anyone makes on anything.

Well, I blame my muddled thinking on Dave. Now here we were, locked in this enterprise together.

The ledge was about five feet down from the opening, and the opposing wall of the cave was only about two feet beyond that, as the two walls came together at the top. So I figured out that if I just slid down with my legs outstretched, I would catch on the other side and be secure. The slide was faster than I thought on that slick, smooth rock. I reminded Dave when it was his turn how extremely important it was to stick his legs out and wedge himself in, as failure to do so meant a twenty-seven-foot plummet. But since he had me to tumble into, it all went fine. Oh, the exhilaration of that lofty perch! We felt like Tolkienesque dwarf kings, yelling down at the flow of humanity sloshing pathetically below on the cave trail.

And then the sobering thought struck. It was the thought that had eluded us all this time. A few brain cells began to light up inside me, and I asked, "How are we going to get down from here?" Dave just stared at me vacuously, and I knew we were doomed. We had slid down to this spot, but given the slipperiness of the ledge, there would be no sliding back up. We tried wedging our way to the right, but quickly discovered that the walls of the cave were getting farther apart. A few panicky moments ticked by, and I struck upon a plan.

"Dave—You're tall. What if you were to climb down me (I've never used that phrase before or since) and hang from my belt? Fully outstretched—hanging from my belt—you'd be, like, seven feet closer to the ground. You could jump to the ground from there, and that'd be like jumping off of a top bunk." Dave agreed, neither of us doing the math to figure out that no bunk bed is twenty feet high. The main point is that Dave agreed, which, once again, was a bad omen.

Dave carefully gripped my belt, and with my back and thighs clenched firmly against the two walls, he swung into a hanging position. While the idiocy of our plan escaped us before, suddenly the hanging Dave became extremely rational. "Hey! This is higher than I thought!" he yelled.

"That may be . . . but there's no turning back now," I countered.

"I think this is too high to jump from." Now all his brain cells were belatedly firing.

"Dave, that would have been a useful thought thirty seconds ago. But now I've got two hundred pounds hanging from my belt. Either jump now by yourself, or wait another minute for me to fall on you!"

Dave realized the clarity of my argument, swallowed hard . . . and let go. I watched him fall and land in an upright position. There. That wasn't so bad. I felt at peace, for about three seconds. Then Dave began to bellow. "I broke my leg!"

"Oh, shut up, wise guy!" He was such a kidder.

"I'm not kidding!" He wasn't kidding. As it turned out, Dave had not broken his leg; he had broken his ankle. At the ER it was later revealed that he had broken his ankle in five places.

The greatest shock belonged to the two guys who happened to be sloshing down the trail about five feet away from Dave's drop point. After the initial terror of seeing a cave troll drop out of the sky in front of them, they regained composure and began to help Dave, one finding a stick for a splint, the other taking a shoelace out to secure the leg. Almost at once I watched while several people appeared from various corners of the cave. It was heartwarming to watch this committee of concerned citizens gather around and slowly hobble Dave outside to a waiting van. And yet this selfish thought persisted in me: "Now what do *I* do?" There went our best plan. And, still—regardless of Dave's condition—I remained all alone at the top of this cave. As the voices disappeared below me, horrible thoughts cropped up. *I'm never coming down. Some park ranger will have to slingshot food to me every day.*

I tried yelling down to passersby for advice. Somebody suggested a rope. (*What rope? Tied to what?*) Another even suggested jumping.

"Already tried that. Thanks."

Most just gave me various versions of "You're never gonna get down!" *Thanks for the encouragement, people.*

No more voices. I began to think of the one who'd gotten me here—that guy Ike from Michigan. *Where was he now?* I began to fantasize about him walking under me so I could plummet on top of him. That would show him. And sure enough, in the solitary blackness of the cave, I heard it—that distinctive Great Lakes accent chatting below.

"Is that Ike?"

A flashlight turned up at me. "Oh! You made it up there, I see."

"Yeah, we made it up here. Thanks for the advice."

"Weren't there a bunch of you?"

"Yeah, there were. One of the guys is on his way to the hospital. There's no way down from here. The ledge was a great idea. Again, thanks."

"Oh, you can get down from there."

"Actually, no I can't. Not slowly, anyway."

"Yeah, you can."

"Why are you so convinced of this?

"I did it earlier today."

Pause. "You did?"

"Yup."

"From here?"

"That exact spot."

"I'm ready to listen." Suddenly, I didn't hate him so much. He told me to wiggle my left leg underneath the ledge where I would find a rock protuberance sufficient to lean my weight on. I followed as he explained, step by step, how to climb from the Ledge of Despair, until I was about seven feet off the ground. I jumped to safety.

I owe Ike a lot. A boring afternoon was transformed into an exciting story that I have related many times over. As for Dave, his ankle cast got him to the front of every line when his family visited Disney World a month later, thus tripling their enjoyment. By the way, if Dave ever agrees with your idea, ditch it immediately.

✝ *The Pastor Says . . .*

I want to start today with a question: Why would anyone want to throw a party in a desert? I'll tell you, but first, have you ever been in a hopeless situation? You may feel like you're in one now.

You may feel trapped in a bad job. You may feel trapped in a dysfunctional relationship. You may feel trapped by poor financial decisions. You may feel trapped in an unhealthy body. You may feel trapped by depression. You may feel trapped on your very own—and very real—"ledge of despair."

If you are sitting on a ledge right now with no apparent way down, I want you to sit tight for just a few more moments while I tell you the story of another group of people who found themselves trapped unexpectedly on a ledge.

The Israelites were God's chosen people, to whom he had promised a land called Canaan. They were on their way to their promised land when they found themselves trapped on a ledge called Egypt.

Egypt was not a nice place to visit—let alone live—for any extended period of time. It was, especially for the Israelites, a place flowing with pain and suffering, but Canaan—the land they were destined for—flowed with blessings as refreshing as milk and sweet as honey. As slaves, forced to build cities for Pharoah, the Israelites faced hard labor, ruthless oppressors, and a dark future. So, they groaned and they cried as they sat, stuck on their "ledge of despair."

Have you ever been there . . . sitting on a "ledge of despair" in darkness so thick no glimmer of hope had any chance of shining through? Do you know what to do when stuck on a "ledge of despair"? Cry out for help.

Yes—despite the darkness—cry out for help.

Despite the fear—cry out for help.

Despite the appearance of complete solitude—cry out for help.

Despite the apparent absence of hope, or help—cry out for help.

God hears.

God heard the Israelites. Moses writes, "The Israelites groaned in their slavery and cried out, and their cry for help because of their slavery went up to God. God heard their groaning . . . and was concerned about them" (Ex. 2:23-25).

Like Ike from Michigan, God will show up at just the right time, and with a better perspective, and shout up . . . I mean . . . down to you, "Oh, you can get down from there."

To which you may reply, "Actually, no, I can't."

To which God will remind you, "Yes, you can."

God is concerned about you. He cares about you, so he wants you to know that there's always a way, there's always a chance, and there's always hope. Sometimes it looks like a guy named Ike, and sometimes it looks like a guy named Moses. Sometimes it requires a leap of faith, and sometimes it requires a forty-year walk through the wilderness, but—with God—there's always hope.

The Israelites cried. God heard.

—Arron Chambers

Spiritual Lessons in Action

Remember a time when you were stuck on a "ledge of despair." List the words that describe how you were feeling on that ledge. Now, take a few moments and detail how God brought you down off that ledge. Pray this prayer: "Lord, thank you for rescuing me. Help me never to forget how it felt to be on that 'ledge of despair' and help me never to forget how great it felt to be rescued. Amen."

A Father Who Knows Best

By Dr. Rebecca Price Janney

J esus continued: "There was a man who had two sons. The younger one said to his father, 'Father, give me my share of the estate.' So he divided his property between them.

"Not long after that, the younger son got together all he had, set off for a distant country and there squandered his wealth in wild living. After he had spent everything, there was a severe famine in that whole country, and he began to be in need. So he went and hired himself out to a citizen of that country, who sent him to his fields to feed pigs. He longed to fill his stomach with the pods that the pigs were eating, but no one gave him anything.

"When he came to his senses, he said, 'How many of my father's hired men have food to spare, and here I am starving to death! I will set out and go back to my father and say to him: Father, I have sinned against heaven and against you. I am no longer worthy to be called your son; make me like one of your hired men.' So he got up and went to his father.

"But while he was still a long way off, his father saw him and was filled with compassion for him; he ran to his son, threw his arms around him and kissed him."

—LUKE 15:11—20

At age twenty-nine, Ting Ting Yan won China's equivalent of an Academy Award, and throughout the 1980s enjoyed celebrity as one of her nation's top novelists and screenwriters. Her hallmark was the innocent story in which people expressed love and kindness, learning how to live purer lives in a corrupt society. She wrote these to create a better life for herself. Although the Communist government rewarded her with a good salary, apartment, and domestic help, the Party demanded total allegiance. "I grew up during Chairman Mao's reign," she says, "and was taught that he was our great father who knew what was best."

"One bitter day when I was fourteen," she recalls, "our school had an assembly. Chairman Mao's minions had roamed the country to weed out all the bad 'seeds' that had taken root." Her father was a teacher, and a Party official had pushed him into a painful crouch. Then he circled Mr. Yan, screeching repeatedly, "You are an enemy of the state!"

In her thoughts Ting Ting repeated, "My father is a good man." She didn't find out until years later that in 1949, her grandfather had been a prominent general who had opposed Chairman Mao. He was executed. Ting Ting's father had removed her grandfather's body from the public square and buried it, and that act had dogged her family for decades.

The Party sent young Ting Ting to a remote farm near Burma for two years to teach Maoism to the peasants. When she finally returned home, she gained admittance into the army's elite dance corps, where she excelled as a performer and worked hard. In spite of her best efforts, however, Ting Ting never got a lead, had to do more menial labor than other dancers, and was forced to sit with new recruits during political classes. The Party leader told her, "Work harder," but no matter what she did, Ting Ting could not remove her family's stain.

One day a younger official asked her if she could write a song for a new production, and he ended up using it for one of the dance routines. That prompted Ting Ting to compose a short story, which the army magazine published. "I grew to love writing," she says. "It gave me some confidence when my self-esteem had plummeted." It was also something that gave her hope after she got kicked out of the army because of her family's political background.

"Afterward, I escaped through writing into a more pleasant world," she says. She did movie reviews for newspapers and magazines, then secured a position with her city's movie studio, producing uplifting documentaries. When the universities reopened in 1978, Ting Ting entered the prestigious Beijing Film Academy. There had been no new movies made in China for ten years, and the government was eager to produce films. The following year, Ting Ting's happiness multiplied when she married a fellow writer. "When I held my dark-eyed daughter Meggie for the first time two years later, I thought my life would continue happily ever after," she says. But then the government ordered Ting Ting and her husband to live in separate cities to keep them available for work. They were allowed one thirty-day visit per year, and the marriage did not survive. The government also required her daughter to reside with Ting Ting's parents so that she could go wherever she was needed.

Ting Ting knew instinctively that life was not supposed to be this way and began a spiritual search that took her initially to the mountains to meet a prominent Buddhist monk.

At one point she asked, "Do you still plant your own vegetables?" Historically monks always had done so. His face suddenly hardened, and his chest puffed out. "I am a level-eighteen government official," he scolded.

Next she went to an ornate Christian church in Beijing, which proved just as disillusioning. "Love your neighbor," the minister proclaimed. "That is what Chairman Mao taught us."

"The Party controls everything," Ting Ting concluded, "even religion." No matter what she did or where she looked, she couldn't make her life like one of her happy stories. Despite the high acclaim her writing had won, she felt hollow.

In March 1989, Beijing University students staged a campus-wide demonstration against government corruption and for democracy. That May, the Tiananmen Square uprising broke out while Ting Ting was working on a new film. She cast her lot with the brave students, remembering all that the government had put her and her family through over the years. "When I marched with the students several miles to the premier's office one hot afternoon," she says, "people lined both sides of the street handing us ice cream and drinks. The love and goodwill I had written about and yearned for manifested itself all around me."

Ting Ting longed to do more. One day she went to the apartment of a celebrated social scientist, Yan Jia-Qi, to see if he had any ideas. He went over to his desk and pulled a petition from a drawer. Ting Ting skimmed the contents of what came to be known as

"The 16th of May Announcement." It asked the government to recognize the legality of the demonstration and not to use violence against the students. It also made a case for promoting democracy and human rights.

"It would help our cause if you signed this," he said. "Think it through, though, since doing so could endanger you." She picked up a pen and signed the document. "For the first time in my life I had no concern about what the Party would think of me," she says.

The petition ran in every important Chinese newspaper, but the government's response was not what its signers desired. Officials ordered tanks to the perimeter of Tiananmen Square, and when the students refused to disperse, the army slaughtered thousands. The government also began searching for intellectuals who had supported the students, including those who had signed Jia-Qi's petition. When the 16th of May Announcement had run in the newspapers, many of the names had been accidentally deleted, and the government started tracking down the missing signers. Ting Ting worried that someone might turn her in. She needed to leave the country, but how? Columbia University accepted her into an English program, and she was able to escape.

Ting Ting faced many challenges in the United States, like not being able to send for her daughter, Meggie, until she could make enough money to support her. Nor could she write for a living because she didn't know English well enough. Later, however, she realized that God was writing his own story about her.

Ting Ting won a grant to study Christian missions in China at Princeton Theological Seminary, but she could not begin until the following fall. In the meantime, she took a temporary position as writer-in-residence at the Presbyterian Conference Center at Stony Point, New York. "Many kind people at the conference center drew me closer to God through their efforts to bring Meggie to me," she says. "In spite of my earlier disappointments with religion, I never had given up on knowing God."

On Father's Day, 1992, Ting Ting attended Stony Point Presbyterian Church. When the pastor, Warner Davis, began his message, Ting Ting half expected a sermon about the virtues of the American system. Instead, he spoke about the importance of fathers. "I dabbed at my tears," she says, "missing my own dad more than ever. I thought of his tortured life and how Father Mao never had accepted me, although I had spent a lifetime trying to please him. As I pondered these things, Pastor Davis referred to God as a Heavenly Father. He said that our earthly fathers often fail us, but God will never leave us or forsake us. He loves us unconditionally."

Tears streamed down Ting Ting's face as the message struck a chord. Wanting to know more about God, she took church membership classes. By Christmas, she had given her life to Christ and was baptized. "Once upon a time, I lived in a world polluted by a man who, though he presented himself as a benevolent father, cared only for himself and his system," she says. "Only in my stories did I experience goodness and mercy. Then I met God, the heavenly Father, who alone had the power to give me a pure life. In his kingdom I have found acceptance by One who forgives generously and loves me lavishly. I call that a real storybook ending!"

✝ *The Pastor Says* . . .

What makes us run? We run to catch the bus. We run to get out of the crosswalk before the traffic light changes. We run to get good seats—up close—at a concert. We run to make ourselves look and feel better. We run to catch a ball, find a ball, dodge a ball, and deliver a ball across a line.

What makes God run? Throughout the Bible we see God doing a variety of things. We see God creating. We see God talking. We see God healing. We see God observing. We see God guiding. We see God forgiving, and throughout the Bible we see God loving, but we see God running only once.

Not that we'd expect to see Him running at all. It's not like He needs to run—at least not for the reasons we typically run. He's everywhere at once, so He's never late. You figure He's too busy running the world to have time to run around it, but, nonetheless, in Luke 15 we see Him running.

So, what makes God run? One day a son wanted his father dead. Well, not exactly, but that's what a son suggests to his father when he asks for his share of the inheritance. A son does not get his share of his father's inheritance until his father is dead. The father agrees and gives his son his share of the estate.

The son who blows through the inheritance in no time finds himself—his Jewish self—feeding pigs, which is about as low as a Jewish man can get. Over time it gets so bad that he longs to eat with the pigs.

Jesus, who's telling this story, says that the young man "came to his senses." Has that ever happened to you? You made a bad choice, found yourself in a bad situation, when, suddenly, the lights came on and you saw your situation and a way out of your situation for the first time.

The son got out of the pigpen and headed home. While he was still a long way from home, his father saw him, felt overwhelming compassion for him, and ran to his son, embracing and kissing him.

The characters in this story, as in all of Christ's parables, represent real people. The youngest son is anyone who is spiritually lost, the eldest son represents the Pharisees, and the father in this story is God.

God, like the father in this parable, is watching for us—hoping to make out our silhouette on the horizon—hoping to recognize our walk, so that he can run out to meet us halfway home. And when he finds us He embraces us, kisses us (which is a sign of acceptance), and then throws a party.

We make God run. Lost people, who have made a turn for home, make God run. He's waiting, He's looking, and He's longing for us to come home. And, lest you think you're too far from home for God to come running after you, remember that He ran from China to New Jersey to show Ting Ting His love.

—Arron Chambers

Spiritual Lessons in Action

Go for a run (this run is not just good for your body—it's also good for your soul), or a fast walk, and, as you run or walk, I want you to say the name of everyone you know who needs to know about God's love. After saying each name, pray that God will give you an opportunity to let that person know how special he or she is to God.

Together

By Kathleen Fuller

They devoted themselves to the apostles' teaching and to the fellowship, to the breaking of bread and to prayer. Everyone was filled with awe, and many wonders and miraculous signs were done by the apostles. All the believers were together and had everything in common. Selling their possessions and goods, they gave to anyone as he had need. Every day they continued to meet together in the temple courts. They broke bread in their homes and ate together with glad and sincere hearts, praising God and enjoying the favor of all the people. And the Lord added to their number daily those who were being saved.

—ACTS 2:42—47

"What do you think about starting our own farm?" My husband posed that unexpected question to me a few years ago as we sat in our matching recliners in the den of our four-bedroom split level in the suburbs.

I pressed the mute button on the TV remote and turned to face him. "A farm?" I asked, trying to decide if his mind had sprung a leak. "You can't be serious."

"It's always been a dream of mine," he said, his tone extremely serious.

"Funny, you never mentioned it to me before."

"I never thought it would be possible before. But lately I've been thinking about it more and more. It would be great to raise a few pigs—"

"Pigs?"

"And cows. Oh, and a bunch of chickens, of course. Wouldn't you like to have fresh eggs every morning?"

"I probably would. Except that I'm not a big fan of eggs."

Ignoring my reply, he went on to explain that if we found the right place, sold our house, and moved to the country, we could have our own subsistence farm, complete with the aforementioned animals. And if everything went according to plan, he could eventually quit his job in the corporate sector and become a gentleman farmer.

I arched a skeptical brow at his idea. "There are a lot of ifs in your scheme, dear," I said, still hanging on to a thin thread of hope that he was toying with me. Suddenly, an image of me standing knee deep in pig slop appeared in my mind. I shoved it away.

"You know what I always say," he replied, grinning. "If you're going to dream, you might as well dream big."

Now, that I could believe. My husband was never one to do anything in a small way. A year later, and after a lot of praying, his dream was set in motion. We found the perfect place in a small, quaint town, sold our house, and moved an hour and a half away from the congested suburbs. All within two weeks. On the outside, I gave him my full support. But secretly I was filled with dread and uncertainty. Our lives would never be the same again.

At the time we were homeschooling our three young children. I had also just embarked on a writing career. In addition, we weren't financially ready to farm full time, so my husband still had his job in the city, which meant a two-hour round-trip commute. What were we getting ourselves into?

As soon as we moved in, my husband began making plans. Grand plans, of course. "Here's where the garden will be," he said to me, gesturing to the large, fenced-in horse pasture. "I'll till it up with my tractor—"

"What tractor?"

"Um, the one I ordered last week," he said quickly, and continued talking before I could say anything else. "The pigs can go there—"

"Back up a minute, cowboy," I said. "Exactly when were you planning to tell me about the tractor?"

"Honey." His voice grew sticky sweet. "Every farmer has to have a tractor."

"I take it the riding lawn mower won't do the job?"

He laughed. "I don't think so. Anyway, we'll put the pigs here, in one of the horse stalls."

I planted my hands on my hips. "How many pigs were you thinking of?" I figured I'd better ask now before he sprung any more surprises on me.

"Ten, for starters." He looked at me and paled slightly. "Okay, how about just three?"

Even three made me nervous, but I agreed anyway. I was determined to be supportive. After all, he wasn't out buying a flashy, expensive sports car or gambling away our life savings in Vegas. All he wanted was a tractor. Some pigs. A few rows of corn. I certainly wasn't about to deny him that.

So we went to work. I helped him divide the pasture and build the pigpen. When the tractor arrived in all its shiny green glory, he began digging up the garden. I brought him water and iced tea to drink, and we picked out seeds together. And when he did bring the little piglets home, I helped him carry them into the pen, high-pitched squeals and all.

But the job of feeding them fell to me. At first I was afraid, and then I was repulsed. Plainly put, pigs stink. They also grow very fast, and are voracious eaters. The phrase "eating like a pig" isn't without a grain of truth. However, as the days and weeks went by, I grew to like them . . . a little. The kids eventually named them Brownie, Cookie, and Chocolate Chip. I would have picked Ham Hock, Tenderloin, and Pork Chop, but that's just me.

A couple of months later it was time to harvest the crops. While my "gentleman farmer" had plowed and planted the garden, it was my job to harvest the vegetables and put them up for winter. Terrified of blowing up the pressure canner and destroying my less than one-year-old kitchen, I opted to freeze all the produce. I believe we could have bought shares of stock in the Ziploc bag company, considering all the baggies I used that fall.

But it wasn't long before I'd had it. At one point I thought if I had to shuck another ear of corn, blanch another beefsteak tomato, or label another one of those plastic freezer bags, I was going to flee screaming out of my kitchen. Instead I took a step back and realized how petty my attitude was. The Lord had blessed us greatly; our cup had truly "runneth" over. And instead of praising Him for His abundance, I was complaining about it. I vowed from that point on to thank God every day, not only for the harvest He gave us, but also for having mercy on my negative outlook.

Eventually fall turned to early winter. The garden was empty, the food was preserved, and the pigs had met their maker. Finally, I thought, we could rest. I was tired, and my body wasn't used to all the physical labor. But I was wrong. We still had a chicken coop to build.

One day in December, as the crisp air turned our noses and cheeks apple red, and as I was holding up a board for my husband to nail into the wall of the coop, it dawned on me that my feelings about what we were doing had changed. I found myself looking forward to the day when we would fill the chicken coop with chicks, pick up three more pigs, and plant an even bigger garden. The idea of making gallons of homemade spaghetti sauce suddenly appealed to me. I was even thinking about conquering my fear of the pressure canner. His dream had become our dream.

"There," my husband said, shooting in the last nail with his heavy-duty nail gun. "It's done." Then he took me in his arms and kissed me on the nose. "I couldn't have done it without you. None of this would have been possible without your help."

Happiness flowed inside me, warming my body and soul more than my dusty, heavy-duty work jacket ever could. How many times had I heard those words from him over the past year?

It was at that moment I realized that this was what marriage was about. Sharing dreams. Celebrating triumphs. Working hard . . . together. We couldn't have done it alone. One of us needed to hold up the board while the other nailed it in. It was as simple as that.

And I knew deep in my heart that it didn't matter how many pigs or chickens we had, or how much work it took to keep the farm going. I was in this for the long haul. We both were. Together.

✝ The Pastor Says . . .

Any time my family was together, my Dad would say it. He said it so much, in fact, that we made a T-shirt for him with the phrase printed across the front. Life is not meant to be lived alone. Being alone against one's will is a tragedy, but so is choosing to be alone. In the beginning God said, "It is not good for the man to be alone" (Gen. 2:18), at the end of his earthly ministry Jesus said, "And surely I am with you always, to the very end of the age" (Matt. 28:20), and when the end comes and eternity begins, we will be gathered together before God's throne (Rev. 7:9).

Sometimes we act as if solitude is heroic. The Lone Ranger was a hero because he single-handedly fought the bad guys. When I was little, I wanted to be the Lone Ranger. I wanted the horse, the gun, the mask, and the heroic solitude, but as I matured I realized that there was nothing heroic about fighting life's battles alone. In fact, I realized that the Lone Ranger wasn't really "Lone." He had a partner, Tonto.

The more I thought about it, the more I realized that most of the cartoon superheroes worked as a part of a team: Batman and Robin, Tarzan and Jane, Buzz Lightyear and Woody, the Fantastic Four, the Three Musketeers, the Justice League, and Fred and Barney (OK, they weren't technically superheroes, but they were pretty super).

And when I started to think about the Bible, I realized that some of the biggest heroes in the Bible worked as part of a team, too: Adam and Eve, Moses and Aaron, Abraham and Sarah, David and Jonathan, Peter and John, Paul and Silas, Jesus and the Twelve Disciples, and the Christian and the Church.

The early Christians were devoted to being together. They didn't come together so they could maintain their listing as a megachurch in their denomination's magazine (even though their 3,000+ numbers would have easily qualified them). They didn't come together because the Jerusalem church had great facilities to meet their every need. They didn't come together to be entertained by a great worship band. They didn't come together to be seen. In fact, being seen with the Church could have meant certain persecution, even death. They didn't have to be convinced, or guilted, into coming together.

No, the early Christians came together because they wanted to be together, they loved being together, and they needed to be together. They were together and their world was being changed. Luke notes that "the Lord added to their number daily those who were being saved."

My Dad loved his family, and every time we gathered together—all of us—he'd say the same thing. It was a saying that encapsulated his feeling about his family being together. In fact, he repeated this saying so much, that we made a T-shirt with his saying written across the front—"It's great to be together."

Yes, it is.

—Arron Chambers

Spiritual Lessons in Action

Plan a date night with your spouse (no kids!), or a night out with a close friend, or lunch with a loved one, and simply enjoy being together.

Light and Darkness

By Melissa Reyes

When Jesus spoke again to the people, he said, "I am the light of the world. Whoever follows me will never walk in darkness, but will have the light of life."

—JOHN 8:12

Three times I've driven at night without my lights on. The first time was the only time I've ever gotten pulled over by a cop. It was late on a Friday night, during spring semester of my junior year at the University of Florida. In addition to taking classes in this fine university and working at this fine university's library, my friend Sydney and I traveled on the weekends and sang in churches, youth groups, and coffee shops. We toted around a hodgepodge of sound equipment and instruments. We scrunched up our faces and squinted our eyes and sang our little hearts out in this genre of acoustic/chill/chick/folk/pop/rock. When it was time to sell our CD, we sheepishly made jokes about how, should our music itself not appeal to the prospective buyer, the CDs still made great coasters and Frisbees, and we clandestinely hoped that some poor soul would take pity on us and support our music through their patronage.

On the trip home from one of these events, we piled our equipment into Sydney's soccer-mom van, facing a two-hour drive. Sydney graciously offered to drive all the way home, so I was able to doze off in the car. We arrived unceremoniously at Sydney's house, where my car had been parked.

Still bleary-eyed, I stumbled into my little white Toyota Corolla for the three quarters of a mile drive to my apartment. I remember passing through an intersection and seeing a police car out of the corner of my eye. I checked my speed: 35 mph. Perfect. I was good to go. I drove on.

In my rearview mirror, I saw the blue lights flashing, clearly signaling me to pull over. I pulled over, 200 yards from my apartment door, and I stared blankly at my steering wheel. I was so tired, I didn't care. The cop approached me.

"Excuse me, miss. Do you know why I pulled you over?"

I stared at him dumbfounded. I knew I hadn't gone over the speed limit. "No."

"Your headlights aren't on."

"They're not?" I was feeling slightly fatigued. I checked the lights. Yep, he was telling the truth. "Oh, yeah." Slight insubordination on my part. I flipped the lights on. "There we go."

"Do you mind if I ask what you're doing, driving around at 1:30 in the morning?"

I explained to him that I was a musician, and that my friend and I were starving artists returning from an extremely posh gig in Orlando, and also, would he like to purchase a CD?

"I hope you weren't the one doing the driving from Orlando!"

I dipped my head sheepishly, glum at my clearly less-than-stellar entrepreneurial skills. "No, sir . . . my friend was driving. Not me."

He snorted. "I should hope so!" He seemed to be thinking. Finally he said, "I'm going to let you off with a warning. Just turn your headlights on."

"Oh, I will, sir. Definitely."

"All right, be safe out there. Remember to drive with them on."

"Thank you, sir."

The second time I drove with my headlights off, I didn't get caught. It was the night before a piano recital that is a requirement for the bachelor of music degree program, and the defining moment of any music major's academic career.

I was driving down a lone road that cut through a national forest. There were no towns, and consequently, no lights for miles. The farther I went, the darker the road seemed to become. I fiddled around with the light and attempted to turn on the high beam.

I must have been distracted thinking about how I'd better hurry home and get a good night's rest, and how tomorrow I was going to either make the folks proud or make good ole Mozart roll in his grave.

I must have been distracted, because I kept on driving, not realizing I had in fact succeeded in turning off my headlights completely, not turning on the high beam as I originally intended. A burst of panic shot adrenaline through me as I realized my error, and then . . . for a brief moment . . . I enjoyed the view.

The sky was blacker, the road seemed more mysterious and promising, and I could've sworn I saw a shooting star or two during that moment of darkness. Then I regained my senses and turned the lights back on. Shooting stars faded away.

The third time I drove without my lights on wasn't my fault. This time, the light that wasn't on was the moon. All the newspapers and anchormen had been reminding us Floridians of the lunar eclipse, which was to occur on Wednesday night.

That night, my friend Amanda and I bought some carrot cake and lattes, piled into her pickup truck, and drove down the highway. We pulled off the road at a place called Payne's Prairie, an enormous tract of swampland that is protected by the government. We enjoyed a soft murmur of anticipation as we looked heavenward. The moon was nearly covered as we sat Indian style in the back of the truck, savoring the carrot cake and coffee.

When the cake and coffee ran out, we lay on our backs and felt small as we stared up at the sky, which was now brilliantly filled with stars that had been outshone by the moon. Tiny, faint points of light emerged as the darkness overtook the moon. Galaxies, previously invisible to the eye, became clear as day.

If anybody knows about darkness, it's Amanda. She has dealt with a rare heart condition ever since she was a kid. I've stood next to her hospital bed after she had just endured eight hours of surgery. I've seen her too sick to move. I've heard her demand that God answer her questions. I've heard her scoff at the story of the prodigal son one minute, then I've witnessed her heart soften in silent understanding in the next. I've heard her act tough and self-reliant, then admit how she yearns to take a leap of faith. I've heard her profess her Thomas-like disbelief, yet offer a prayer of thanks to God for simple things like lattes, and music, and lunar eclipses. Darkness . . . then light.

But on the night of the eclipse her deep love for God was as clear as the North Star. That night, I suddenly remembered the times I had prayed that she would see a glimpse of God in our friendship;

that she would somehow align her heart with that of the Father; that her heart would respond to the overtures that He was constantly, consciously making toward her. I remembered periods of frustration and defeat and . . . well . . . darkness. I also remembered how good it felt to see the light turned back on.

Darkness had unveiled my eyes to witness the swirl of galaxies and God's creation from billions of light-years away. Darkness had inspired me to take light a lot more seriously.

I don't know why God allows Amanda's darkness to be so much more painful and last so much longer than mine. I don't know why she gets hospitals, doctors, bad news, sleepless nights, and bottles of medication, while I get paper cuts.

I don't know why my darkness lasts for a second on a lonely road, and then I get to see a shooting star. Maybe God gives us each what we can handle . . . . Maybe that's why I get one star and Amanda gets an entire galaxy.

✝ *The Pastor Says . . .*

We all face times of darkness. Like the night that visits us every twenty-four hours, some people are visited regularly by darkness, but unlike the night of which we are so familiar, others are visited by an extended period of darkness that may last for days, weeks, even years.

No light switch and no rising sun can remove some of the darkness in which some of you find yourselves. The only way out is to follow the Light.

I was at a bonfire eighteen years ago last July. It was on the southwest shore of Yellowstone Lake in Yellowstone National

Park. What was supposed to be an innocent gathering of friends after work quickly became something quite different when a group of rowdy guys—who had not been invited—showed up with a lot of alcohol and some drugs. Those of us who had planned the gathering were very uncomfortable. I decided it was time for me to go and turned to leave, only to find a darkness that looked impassable.

I had a choice to make: stay in the darkness of sin, or step into the darkness of night. I chose to wade into the darkness away from the fire. As I left the glow of the firelight, I could not see my hand in front of my face, but I pressed on. There was no moonlight, no streetlight, and I had no flashlight. I slowly and carefully felt my way back to the path. As my feet touched the path I noticed a light in the distance. It was the light on the corner of the parking lot for my dorm. I fixed my gaze on that light and walked toward it. I made it home, vowing never to get myself into that situation again.

Like Melissa, I found that darkness had inspired me to take light a lot more seriously. I won't drive, or live, without the lights on.

—Arron Chambers

Spiritual Lessons in Action

Go into a dark room or a closet and, in the darkness, confess your sins to the Lord. Be specific, because He is big enough—and good enough—to handle our shortcomings. Ask for His forgiveness. When you are finished, leave the darkness, and resolve to live the rest of this day—and your life—in the light.

Kaitlyn's Gift

By Kim Vogel Sawyer

T his is how we know what love is: Jesus Christ laid down his life for us. And we ought to lay down our lives for our brothers. If anyone has material possessions and sees his brother in need but has no pity on him, how can the love of God be in him? Dear children, let us not love with words or tongue but with actions and in truth.

—JOHN 3:16—18

"Mommy, what is that talking about?" I looked over the edge of the kitchen counter to my daughter, who pointed at the television. A commercial played, advertising the 1993 Toys for Tots campaign.

Coming around the counter to stand beside her, I explained. "Those soldiers are asking for people to give toys to them. Then, on Christmas Eve, they'll give the toys to boys and girls who otherwise wouldn't get any presents for Christmas."

Kaitlyn's blue eyes widened as she peered up at me in dismay. "Some kids don't get presents?"

I shook my head, smoothing her wispy blonde hair from her face. "That's right, pumpkin. Some kids aren't as lucky as you."

I watched Kaitlyn process this information. Small for her age, having come into the world a bit ahead of schedule, Kaitlyn had nonetheless always had a big heart. I could see she was troubled at the thought of children not receiving Christmas presents. To reassure her, I said, "Don't worry about it, sweetheart. That's why they have Toys for Tots—to make sure nobody gets left out at Christmastime."

That night, as Kaitlyn said her bedtime prayers, she added a post-script: "And God, about those kids who don't get presents. Could you make sure people give a whole bunch of toys so every kid will get a Christmas present?"

Every night for the next two weeks, Kaitlyn made that same prayer. My heart thrilled at the tenderness being expressed through her innocent prayer, and I found myself sending up the same petition when I went to bed at night.

On December 10, a week before Kaitlyn's seventh birthday, she hopped through the door after school and pulled herself onto the breakfast barstool for her snack. Her mouth full of peanut butter cookies, she asked, "Mommy, can I invite my whole class to my birthday party?"

"Everybody? Not just the girls?"

"No. I want the girls and the boys, too."

I sent her a teasing wink. "Oh, I know why you want lots of kids at your party."

She sat up straight, her expression expectant. "You do?"

"Mm-hm. You just want lots of birthday presents."

Immediately her little face clouded. She climbed down from the stool and disappeared into her bedroom. Assuming I had hurt her feelings in some way, I followed her. She sat on the edge of her bed, her head down.

I sat down beside her and put my around her small shoulders. "What's the matter, pumpkin?"

Kaitlyn looked up at me. Tears glistened in the corners of her eyes, making her sky blue eyes appear even brighter. "I don't want any more presents for me. I have lots of toys already. But can I ask my friends to bring a present for that Toys for Tots thing?" For a moment, she seemed uncertain. "I prayed for God to give those kids toys. Do you think it's okay if I help?"

Tears stung my eyes as I gave Kaitlyn a hug. "Honey, I think God would be delighted for you to help." I knew the Toys for Tots campaign was nearing its end. I wasn't sure if they would still collect toys after Kaitlyn's birthday. "Do you want me to call and find out if the soldiers need some more toys?"

She nodded with enthusiasm. "Yes!"

Kaitlyn was at school the next day. I called the Army Reserves Armory in nearby McPherson, the nearest collection point.

"We generally don't receive toys after December 16, ma'am," the voice on the other end of the line told me.

My heart sank. Kaitlyn's birthday was the 17th, and if we had her party on her birthday as we'd planned, we wouldn't be able to deliver the toys until December 18. I couldn't bear facing my daughter's disappointment. Breathing a silent prayer, I asked, "Could you possibly make an exception?" I explained what Kaitlyn wanted to do. The voice asked if I could hold, and it seemed I waited an interminable amount of time until someone returned to the telephone.

"Ma'am? What time could you be here on the 18th?"

"Not until after five, probably," I said, almost holding my breath.

There was another pause as I prayed inwardly—Please, God, please, please. Kaitlyn will be so crushed—and finally the person said, "I tell you what. I'll stick around that afternoon so I can let you in."

"Oh, thank you." My breath whooshed out with the words. "And bless you!"

Together, Kaitlyn and I designed birthday invitations. In crayon, Kaitlyn painstakingly wrote on the bottom of each invitation, "Bring one unwrapped gift for a boy or girl for Toys for Tots (not for Kaitlyn)." She followed that line of instruction with a smiley face.

She handed the invitations to every classmate during recess at school the next day. At suppertime, I asked if her friends were excited about her party.

"They all want to come, Mommy! That means seventeen presents." Then she paused, her brow furrowed. "But it will be eighteen if I buy a present, too."

I laughed. "Okay, we'll buy you a present, too, to give away."

She grinned her thanks.

The day of her party, Kaitlyn squealed with delight at every toy that was carried through the door. She deposited the cars, dolls, coloring books, games, and stuffed animals in big boxes, which we had decorated with Christmas wrapping paper and bows. With each delivery, she announced, her eyes shining, "Won't those kids be surprised?"

The day after her birthday, she and I loaded the boxes into the back of our van and drove to the Armory. Three volunteers greeted us.

"Hello!" Kaitlyn chirped, beaming her toothless smile as she bounced through the doors with her arms full. "Look! These are my birthday presents, but you can have them. They're for those kids for Christmas." She hummed as she helped the volunteers arrange her gifts on tabletops scattered with every variety of toy.

Kaitlyn walked between the rows of tables, pointing to the piles of unwrapped toys, her blue eyes wide with wonder. "Look at all these presents, Mommy. I bet every kid gets a present now."

"I'll bet you're right, pumpkin." How it lifted my heart to see Kaitlyn in action, her joy so obvious at the opportunity to give.

Before we left, Kaitlyn gave each of the volunteers a hug and wished them a merry Christmas. All the way home, she jabbered about what she'd seen—the abundance of toys awaiting delivery to boys and girls. She seemed awed by the number of presents. "Where did they all come from?" she asked.

"Well, just like you gave presents, other people gave presents, too. Lots of people brought in toys for those boys and girls."

She nodded, satisfied with my answer. That night, when she knelt for her prayers, she said, "God, thank you for the people who gave all those toys. Give them a hug for me, would you, please? And thank you that all the boys and girls will have a good Christmas now."

When I went to bed that night, I gave God thanks, too—for the others who had generously given so a needy child might enjoy a gift on Christmas morning, but mostly for Kaitlyn, my precious little girl who could see beyond selfishness to the joy of giving. "God, bless Kaitlyn."

✝ The Pastor Says . . .

Perhaps you've heard the saying, "That's easier said than done." So many things in life are easier said than done:

"Dad, I want to learn how to ride my bike."

"When I grow up I want to be a doctor."

"Let's get married."

"Let's have a baby."

"I'm going to start exercising tomorrow morning."

"I think it's time for us to start going to church, again."

"Yes, your parents can stay with us for a month this summer."

"I love you."

Love is easier said than done. Fifteen years ago, I stood at the altar, looked at my lovely bride, and said, "I love you." I didn't realize it at the time, but that was the easy part—saying "I love you."

Doing "I love you" is hard work and sometimes not that fun. Doing "I love you" requires sacrifice, patience, compromise, communication, selflessness, serving, commitment, in-laws, saying "I'm sorry," and changing diapers when it's your turn!

Knowing this, the Apostle John points to Jesus as the perfect example of doing "I love you." John says, "This is how we know what love is: Jesus Christ laid down his life for us." Jesus spoke a message of love each day of his life, but never was his love as clearly communicated as it was on the cross. Christ's words about love—his stories, his sermons, his prayers—describe love clearly, but his death defined true love once and for all time.

Saying "I love you," is easy—it doesn't require sacrifice, effort, time, commitment, a marriage license, a cross, or a birthday party for needy kids.

But, doing "I love you" makes us more like Jesus . . . and Kaitlyn.

—Arron Chambers

Spiritual Lessons in Action

Do something for someone that shows that you love them.

The Baseball and the Song

By John H. Smith

Moses answered, "What if they do not believe me or listen to me and say, 'The LORD did not appear to you'?" Then the LORD said to him, "What is that in your hand?" "A staff," he replied. The LORD said, "Throw it on the ground."

—EXODUS 4:1–3

How far back can one remember? Why does one thing remain in memory when so many other things are forgotten?

It may be that certain events are embedded in our minds because they are firsts. There are often consequences from firsts, which result in life-changing pursuits. Most of us can remember the first day of school, the first love, and maybe the first birthday party.

Being a minister, I certainly remember my first sermon. I have tried to forget it, but it is burned into my memory. I have four children, and I love them in equal measure; but I must confess that I remember the details of my firstborn better than that of the others. Firsts are very important, but so are seconds and thirds . . . but we just don't seem to remember them as well.

I want to tell you about my first baseball. Little did I know then that my first baseball would set my life on a course that I have never regretted, and it would not be a life in sports.

I was four years old when my father moved his family to Elizabethton, Tennessee. The year was 1945. Being a minister, he had accepted the ministry at First Christian Church in Elizabethton. The world war was over, and people were settling down to a simple and peaceful life. I began public school in that sleepy little town, and my school was within walking distance of the parsonage where we lived on H Street.

I played with many friends on that street. We had a wonderful time with our clubs and sporting competitions, like baseball.

Our baseball field was really a field. We had no real bases or fancy equipment. Times were hard and money was short in the late forties, and so I had limited sporting equipment to use in these games. I surely did not have a real baseball to use.

It isn't always easy being a preacher's kid. I was often taken to church fellowship parties with my mother. There were no kids my age at these gatherings. I would rather have been with my friends out there on H Street playing ball; but unfortunately, circumstances were such that I had to go to many of these church activities.

One of my life-changing events took place at one of these socials. I became like a mascot to these young married couples at these fellowship meetings. They kidded, teased, and played with me, and, I must admit, I enjoyed the attention. Ed "Bulldog" Laws and his beautiful wife, Martha, were present at one of these fellowship meetings. Although I did not know it at the time, Ed was a great football hero in our community. Ed had excelled in sports at Elizabethton High School, had continued his career at Baylor University, and had finished at Milligan College.

I remember so vividly how Ed took a special liking to me that night. I was probably about seven or eight years old at this time. Ed kept pressing me to sing a song for him. I had never sung a song before, and besides, I was very backward and shy at this age. He finally made an offer to me.

He said, "If you will sing me a song, I will give you a brand new major-league baseball."

What an offer for a young kid!

I was, however, in a negotiating mood. I said I would do it if we could go by ourselves into a Sunday School room and if I could stand with my back to the door of the room. Ed Laws and the rest of the adults could stand at the door and listen, but I needed privacy.

Well, the adults agreed to my terms, and I began sweating. We got into our positions, and I sang my rendition of "O My Darling, Clementine."

They were kind to applaud my feeble effort. Then Ed went out to his car and brought to me a brand new major-league baseball. I was so thrilled to receive it. It was my first baseball. I treasured that ball and used it all through the years of my youth. I still had that ball when I finally went off to college, but it has since been lost.

I did not know when I received that baseball that Ed "Bulldog" Laws would not live very long after this encounter. He died very suddenly of an aneurysm, a young man of twenty-seven. Each year at our local high school, the Ed "Bulldog" Laws Award is given to the most outstanding football player.

I often thought of Ed as I played with that baseball throughout the years. The baseball was a great gift, but it wasn't the only gift he gave me that night. That night, at the church social in a secluded Sunday School classroom, I sang my first solo, but it would not be my last. I developed my singing voice and used it in my church work these past forty-three years. I have preached and sung in many congregations, in revivals, in weddings, and in funerals all over the country. I even do Sermons in Song that I use in revival meetings and special services.

I have often wondered what would have happened if a famous athlete had not challenged a shy child to sing that solo so long ago. But he did and it changed my life.

Some day, I hope to thank Ed in person for showing an interest in me—a clumsy and backward boy—and for giving me that baseball that led to a song that led to a ministry.

✝ *The Pastor Says* . . .

God loves to get the credit, that's why He loves to do amazing things with ordinary things. He loves to do a lot with a little. He loves when our jaws drop in amazement as we witness His power.

God could have arranged for Goliath to be killed by another giant, but he chose to let him die at the hands of a shepherd boy, a sling, and a stone (I Samuel 17). Why? God wants us to know that He can do a lot with a little.

Jesus could have healed the blind man with flashing lightning, flying angels, and a lot of fanfare, but he chose to heal the blind man with mud balls made with spit (John 9). Why? God wants us to know that He can do a lot with a little.

Jesus could have let the 5,000 people stay hungry, but he chose to feed them with only five loaves of bread and two fish (Matthew 14:13–21). Why? God wants us to know that He can do a lot with a little.

A sling in David's hand changed a shepherd boy.

A mud ball in the hand of Jesus changed a blind man.

A sack lunch in Jesus' hand changed a meal.

And a baseball in Ed Laws's hand changed a boy.

What will you do with what's in your hand?

—Arron Chambers

Spiritual Lessons in Action

Go to a sports store and buy a baseball. On the baseball, I want you to list your talents—as many as you can think of—and then, as you hold the baseball in your hand, pray this prayer: "Lord, I know that you can do a lot with a little. These are the talents you've given to me. Take them and use them for your purposes. I want to make a difference in this world. Lord, take my life and my talents and use them to change this world. Amen."

Lessons from My Backyard

By Leigh-Angela Holbrook

T herefore, since we are surrounded by such a great cloud of witnesses, let us throw off everything that hinders and the sin that so easily entangles, and let us run with perseverance the race marked out for us.

—HEBREWS 12:1

I love the smell of fresh-cut grass on a Saturday morning, especially if I'm not the one cutting it. This particular Saturday morning, the odds were not in my favor.

The day started out exactly the way I like it: on the back of a horse. I was sweaty and disgusting and completely happy to be out enjoying the Texas heat. As I walked back up to the house, it was becoming clear that all of the rain we'd had this week, which had been such a blessing, left the grass needing to be cut, again.

With my husband on a two-week trip and my son in the house running a fever, the pleasure would have to be all mine.

Now, over the years, I've come to make the best of the time while I mow by treating the time as a kind of prayer walk on wheels. Our little place in Magnolia has about one and a half acres that require attention, while my horse takes care of the rest. That many acres allows for lots of prayer, in theory. My adventure begins with a run around the fence line.

"Thank you Lord, for this beautiful place in the country. It's been such a blessing. . . . ."

Hey, there's my new neighbor Peg. "Hey, Peg!" *Wonder if we're going to be friends. Hmm.* "Dear Lord, please bless my friendship with Peg as we grow to know each other."

There's my horse, Bugzy. "Hey, Bug man! Good boy!"

"Thank you Lord for answering the prayers of a little girl who grew up to still love horses. Thank you so."

Hey, was that an extension cord I just ran over? I look behind me. Yes, but, whew, no harm done. This is the extension cord that is temporarily supplying the electric fence with zapping power to keep my favorite dog in the yard.

Oh, there's the mail lady! "Hey mail lady!" *There goes stupid white dog chasing the mail lady.* "Thank you, Lord, that I still have stupid white dog and that the zapping wire is keeping her safely in her yard. "

Hey, what about that cord? Yeah, I passed over it again. But I realize I won't have to stop and deal with it.

There's my son's tree house. "Thank you, Lord, for Jeff and Hunter and the great relationship they have. That fort is a symbol of so much that they've done together."

And so it goes . . . in and out of the shade . . . round the giant black walnut trees with the long-hanging moss. Up and down . . . back and forth . . . prayers and rambling thoughts.

Suddenly . . . Wham! Clank! . . . sparks . . . Thunk! The mower is sickeningly silent. The extension cord now requires my attention. I've managed to split it and suck it up in to the bowels of the mower. So, now it's time to drag my tired sweaty self into the house to unplug the remnant of the cord.

Somewhere under the mower lies the consequence of my laziness. Now to master the hydraulic jack, lift the mower, and get to the source of the problem. Not happening. Not even close. I'm a Texas woman. I should be able to figure this out. This self-respecting Texas woman sheepishly asks her sick son to please come help.

After two attempts, one of which involves lying in a pile of fire ants, we lift the mower and I am rewarded with a magnificent abstract design of weeds and extension cord artfully wrapped and knotted around each blade over and over. Round and round. Up and down. Back and forth. Entangled.

My sweet son helped without stating the obvious. I could have avoided a huge mess had I not been too lazy to clear the yard of all that would have slowed me down or tripped me up.

After running out of gas, cooling down the mower, and refilling it with gas, I collapsed in the kitchen, only to realize that I had tripped a breaker and had no fans or lights.

Note to self: Next time, this self-respecting Texas woman will sip iced tea from the safety of the porch swing and watch the menfolk tend to the yard.

✝ *The Pastor Says . . .*

Don't ask me how I know, but it's difficult to run in a long dress. To move quickly in a dress, one must pull up the bottom of the dress and hold it—not too high—in your hands, freeing up room for the legs to do what they were designed to do. Neglecting to do this may result in your tumbling across a stage in front of a lot of friends, classmates, school officials, and other witnesses who are now laughing uncontrollably as you struggle to gather up your dignity and get offstage. Don't ask me how I know.

The ancients, who wore robes, called this process, "Girding up." When God is trying to prepare Jeremiah for his special ministry he says, "Now, *gird up* your loins and arise, and speak to them all which I command you. Do not be dismayed before them, or I will dismay you before them" (Jeremiah 1:17, NAS, emphasis mine). Soldiers would tuck the bottom of their robes into their belt so they could move freely and swiftly.

Nothing as trivial as a dress should be allowed to trip us up and keep us from doing what needs to be done.

The author of Hebrews is writing to an audience who is mostly Jewish. They are now believers in Christ, so he is encouraging them to hold on to their newfound faith in Christ, instead of going back to their old belief system. In chapter eleven of Hebrews, the writer lists some of the heroes of their faith: Noah, Abraham, Sarah, Moses, Rahab, and others who survived this life with their faith in God intact.

Then, immediately, the author of Hebrews—before the memories of these faithful men and women can fade into the recesses of readers' minds—writes, "Therefore, since we are surrounded by such a great cloud of witnesses." These "witnesses" lived faithful lives, not perfect lives. They made mistakes, but they didn't allow the mistakes to keep them from fulfilling the plan God had for their lives. This awareness should sustain us when we feel like quitting. There are many faithful people who have made it and are rooting for us to make it, too.

We must keep our lives free from anything that might "hinder" and "entangle" us, causing missteps and embarrassment in front of both faithful and unfaithful witnesses. Sin is not funny; it's deadly. We are in a race and we must finish, because losing awards a horrible trophy. Let's keep our lives pure, so our movements can be swift, free, and faithful.

Remember, it's difficult to mow with an extension cord wrapped around your blade; it's difficult to run in a long dress; and it's difficult to live for Christ while entangled in sin.

Don't ask me how I know.

—Arron Chambers

Spiritual Lessons in Action

Sit down in a comfortable place with this book and wrap your legs loosely with a belt or a piece of rope. As you sit with your legs entangled, reflect on the choices you've made that have hindered your walk with the Lord. As you unwrap your legs I want you to pray this prayer: "Lord, I refuse to let anything keep me from walking with you. I will not allow myself to be entangled. I will not allow myself to be tripped. I will not allow myself to be stopped. I will do whatever it takes to walk with you—unhindered—every wondrous day of my life. Amen."

Getting Hitched

By Serenity Johnson

T hen I heard what sounded like a great multitude, like the roar of rushing waters and like loud peals of thunder, shouting: "Hallelujah! For our Lord God Almighty reigns. Let us rejoice and be glad and give him glory! For the wedding of the Lamb has come, and his bride has made herself ready."

—REVELATION 19:6,7

Getting married isn't all it's cracked up to be. The last month of preparation is when all the best-laid plans and excitingly original ideas turn into a mess of hurt feelings and egos. Wedding decorations become as equally neglected as they are necessary, and you finally bog down in a confusing myriad of lists about lists for the lists you were going to make when you heard the list of reasons why lists were the best way to go about planning a party that should be thrown in your honor.

Six months prior to the storm before the ultimate calm, I had unwittingly and euphorically said "yes" (or something more to the effect of—"Is this when I say 'yes'?") to an altogether pleasant and nervous young man offering me a ring of his choosing from the six or seven I'd merely hinted at in the brochure replete with printouts I'd put together. We put off our first order of business, the calling of the list (a first of many) of essential friends and relatives, until after a celebratory dinner.

Shortly after our engagement, we went to his hometown of Cincinnati, whereupon we were lavished with congratulations from equally excited relatives, the sum of which formed what I would soon lovingly refer to as "my in-laws."

Then, engaged for less than a month, I went dress shopping with my future mother-in-law, a feat I was wholly unprepared to conquer. For a month or so before the engagement happened, I—together with my roommates—had been poring over Web sites investigating dress types and shapes and sizes, enthralled by the world of couture. I had a general idea of certain desirable features, but certainly not an idea clear enough, sure enough, and settled enough for an $800 investment at this time. His mom took me to the biggest bridal salon in all of the country, overwhelming to say the very least.

Upon filling out an information card, we were greeted by Shelia, who treated the process like routine surgery. We were to "pull," or choose, seven dresses from the thousands of white costumes staring us down in various shades of white. In paying heed to the subtleties of our every move, Shelia too would pick out three or four. She both sweetly and humbly informed us that she would probably end up pulling my wedding gown. My mother-in-law and I later confessed to one another that our initial reaction had been "Yeah, right."

In several hours, not only my idea of the kind of dress I liked, but also, it seemed, my basic perceptions of the world had, more or less, been turned upside down, most likely due to information and decision-making overload. I'd never given my opinion so many times and in so many words in all of my life. I had put on beaded things and actually liked them, lacy things and realized how heavy and itchy they were, flowy things and learned about the necessity that the dress match the mood of the wedding. At last, I put on a two-piece corset top, combined with a chapel-length skirt made out of gathered organza, complete with a designer's name heralding its quality. It was picked out by Shelia, no less, and only days later I charged it to my Visa.

While in Ohio, my fiancé and I planned most of the wedding details. When I say "most," what I mean is what a normal person not versed in wedding etiquette would perceive to be most. Choosing colors was more fun than labored (except for what to rename green and purple so they sounded witty and informed). The table arrangements came quickly, and the decision of our attendants had long been understood. CDs came to mind as cheap and easy-to-personalize favors. My husband would even design the invitations from the genius of his very own computer-savvy mind. "Do it yourself" and crafts were to abound. With all the apparent ease of wedding planning, newly engaged bliss ensued!

Five months later came that last and most terrible month, prefaced by the addressing and sending of invitations. I turned into a cantankerous bride-to-be. Suddenly, it seemed, my fiancé was asking stupid questions that I deemed too unworthy to warrant any polite response. His resulting confusion only fanned the interminable flame. With the threat of summer vacation looming ever swifter on the horizon, my maid of honor and I couldn't make candle centerpieces fast enough. Envelopes started coming back stamped by the post office as "undeliverable." And then school let out.

I moved to the home of one of my roommates, an hour and $3.50 in tolls away from my fiancé. To make matters inexorably worse, a month before the wedding, my best college friends and I had planned a week-and-a-half-long graduation road trip. I put away the stresses for ten days, only to be greeted with them in fuller force upon return.

The last week of my single life I was driving that two hours a day and paying $7 in tolls every day and getting home after one in the morning. The hair and makeup appointments had fallen through, and my maid of honor and I went to every hair salon within a half-hour radius, the week before the event, desperately trying to secure appointments for eight formal hairdos.

Having decided to do the flowers myself, their delayed delivery on the day before the wedding was met with a fair degree of dissatisfaction. Speaking of the day before the wedding, my almost-husband and I decided to have a late lunch with our immediate families on Friday. Lasting nearly three hours, this final farewell turned out to be an ill-fated idea. Traffic was so bad that I barely made it to the rehearsal at the prescribed time.

Speaking of the rehearsal, when I got to the church, five or so minutes late, the sanctuary was filled with nothing but stacked chairs. I was asked if I'd like them set up. I responded that, yes, I would, in fact, appreciate the assembly of at least an aisle in order to enable the practice of a wedding, in which aisles are all but mandatory. The only hitch I was interested in was becoming hitched myself.

Speaking of hitches, my attendants and I were up until two in the morning wrapping CDs, making bouquets, exchanging gifts, not watching a movie we'd rented specifically for the occasion, and running last-minute errands until fatigue overcame us. Four hours later, my maid of honor and her mother and sister woke up, and we met my future husband to finish decorating the reception space. After scrambling across counties to hair appointments, I learned that my already rescheduled makeup appointment had also fallen through, so I wandered through a mall in someone else's pajamas, begging anyone who might care to paint some sort of happiness onto my bridal face. Luckily, someone unhappily obliged. With twenty minutes to spare, a kindly Vietnamese woman manicured mine and my mother's nails.

With the beginning of the pre-ceremony music, my attendants and I snuck into the hall to hear the proficient pianist play. The hitches had stopped coming, my dad said good-bye and made me cry, we walked down the aisle, and with some vows and feet washing, I found myself married.

Of course, the work of a wedding isn't done until the bubbles are blown. As a wife with a husband, I stayed for the remaining festivities of the most talked about and tediously planned day and evening of my entire life. Along with easy company was food—abundant and good—matched by a tasty, albeit slightly melted, cake. The details no longer mattered. The invitations were long forgotten. The candles were melting into oblivion. The toiled-over CDs had been opened, their wrappings thrown away. Fourteen hours after I had awoken, my parents drove my husband and me to his bachelor apartment to unload the fruits of our labor (presents, of course!) en route to the hotel. Hugging, then waving good-bye, he and I, with exhausted sighs, began the task of settling into a vastly different life.

Getting married certainly wasn't all it was cracked up to be. Don't misunderstand, the getting married is what failed to meet my inflated expectations; the being part, however, is a newly ventured and profoundly enjoyable expedition.

✝ *The Pastor Says . . .*

Weddings are beautiful—but not realistic.

My father and mother conducted many seminars on family life. During these seminars, my father would paint the following picture of what a wedding would look like if it were more realistic. If weddings were more realistic, the wedding would take place in the TV room with the TV left on throughout the entire ceremony, since that appears to be the setting and environment for a lot of marriages. Both families would be onstage with the bride and groom, which seems appropriate to me, since both families will be in the marriage.

The groom would not be wearing a tuxedo but an old pair of shorts—replete with both holes and stains from odd jobs from days gone by—a ratty T-shirt, and dark socks with holes in the toes. He'd be holding a remote throughout the ceremony.

The kids would be in the ceremony, or should I say, around the room, or should I more accurately say, running around the room not using their "inside" voices.

The bride would not be wearing a lovely white gown, but a bathrobe and fuzzy slippers. Her straggly hair would be pulled back in a scrunchy, she'd have some type of green cream on her face, and she'd be crying for no apparent reason. She'd have a baby on her hip and, of course, the baby would be in need of changing.

As they left, the new couple would be pelted—not with rice—but with dirty laundry.

And when the ceremony was over, they would be charged $1000 they didn't know about in advance.

I'm glad weddings aren't realistic. Life is hard, and every couple deserves to start their lives together with dancing—being dressed well, toasted, well fed, and surrounded by the most important people in their lives, but it takes a lot of work to prepare for a typical wedding ceremony.

I'm always amazed at how much work the bride and her family have to do to get ready for the big day: reserve a location for the ceremony and another for the reception, order a dress for the bride, pick out dresses for the bridesmaids, pick out flowers, hire a photographer, meet with the wedding coordinator, counsel with the minister, select a cake, send out invitations, find a caterer, and much more.

Likewise, I'm always amazed at how little work the typical groom does. It's been my experience that the typical groom is expected to do only one thing: show up.

What if the bride did that? What if the bride decided just to show up? The wedding would end up being . . . realistic.

In this revelation to John, we hear the multitudes in heaven shouting their praises to God announcing the wedding of the ages. The groom is Jesus—the Lamb—and the bride is the church. The groom is going to do what He's expected to do: show up. And according to the last chapter of the book of Revelations, he will be "coming soon" (Rev. 22:7,12,20). The Groom is on his way. He's doing what he's supposed to do.

Today may be the big day. Are we doing what we're supposed to do? I can't wait. Our wedding with the Lamb is going to be unreal!

—Arron Chambers

Spiritual Lessons in Action

Make a list of the top ten things you would do if you had only one year left to live. How is this list different from what you are doing now? Does this list reflect different priorities than your current to-do list? Above the list, write "Jesus is coming soon!" Make this list your new to-do list!

Run for Daddy

By Tamara J. Davis

D o you not know that in a race all
the runners run, but only one gets
the prize? Run in such a way as to
get the prize. Everyone who competes in the
games goes into strict training. They do it to
get a crown that will not last; but we do it to
get a crown that will last forever. Therefore I
do not run like a man running aimlessly; I do
not fight like a man beating the air. No, I beat
my body and make it my slave so that after I
have preached to others, I myself will not be
disqualified for the prize.

—I CORINTHIANS 9:24–27

I was always a daddy's girl. It was Dad who
taught me how to throw a football, swing
a bat, and bait a hook and, like most daddy's
girls, where Dad was, I wanted to be. Since my
Dad was a runner, that meant I spent many
Saturday mornings watching him race. For a
girl who usually had to be pulled out of bed

every morning, I was amazingly eager to wake up at the crack of dawn on Dad's race days. Sometimes the whole family went along, but every once in a while it was just Dad and me.

I couldn't imagine letting him work so hard to cross the finish line with no one there to cheer him on. At the start of a race, I would stand at the sidelines, squinting against the morning sun to find my dad among the crowd of runners. I'd frantically wave and scream, "Go, Dad, go!" even though he couldn't see or hear me. But my favorite part of the day was waiting at the finish line.

I refused to take my eyes off the runners making their way down the final stretch, afraid that if I did, I might miss Dad. Upon first glimpse of him sprinting to the finish, I would cup my hands to my mouth and cheer at the top of my lungs: "Come on, Dad! Go! You can do it! Go, Dad!" I wanted everyone to hear me cheering Dad on. It was as if I were saying, "See that tall, skinny guy coming toward us? That's my dad!"

The tables were slightly turned during my eighth-grade year when I joined the school track team. I wanted to run because Dad ran, and I knew Dad would be thrilled with my decision to compete in a sport he loved. That first week of practice seemed grueling, and I wondered what I had gotten myself into. Each day at the start of practice we had to run a mile, and for the first few days my scrawny legs ached with every step I took.

I began to wonder why my dad, or any human being for that matter, would voluntarily submit their bodies to such punishment. Eventually, though, my aching body adjusted, and I began looking forward to practice and what I might accomplish that day. I would come home and excitedly share the events of the day and wait for Dad's response. "That's good, honey," he'd say, or "Now, don't push yourself too hard." He'd give me advice on warming up, stretching out, how to pace myself, and the stance I should take when starting a race. It felt good talking to Dad runner to runner, and I took every word of his advice to heart.

Not long into the season, we had a track meet that I was particularly excited about. I would be running my favorite race, the 220-yard dash, and I knew Dad would be in the stands watching. I wanted him to see me win a race, and I felt like I had a chance with this one. During warmups before the meet began, I felt a slight sting in the back of my right thigh as we stretched out, but I quickly put it out of my mind.

Later on, as I sat on the sidelines with my teammates, I anxiously awaited my race. When we were finally called out to the track, I immediately felt my heart pounding in my chest and my throat tightening. *Calm down,* I thought. *It's just a race.* But as I stood at the line for what seemed like ages, waiting to hear the starting gun, I could only think two profound words over and over in my mind. *Run fast. Run fast. Run fast.* Then I heard, "On your mark! Get set!" and the gun blasted. "Run fast, run fast, run fast!" I told myself as my momentum almost toppled me head over feet.

I got control and, as we rounded the curve, I felt myself pulling out in front. I could hear the other girls, their feet pounding against the track at what sounded like inches behind me. When I was just a few feet from the finish line I thought, *OK. This is it I'm gonna win this thing.* The moment that thought was leaving my mind, my right leg gave out underneath me, and I stumbled to the ground. Out of the corner of my eye I could see the other girls crossing the finish line. I was sick with disappointment. Seconds after I fell, my coach ran over to me and gently lifted me up into her arms. As she carried me across the line, I looked up and saw my dad standing there.

I never asked Dad how he got down from the bleachers to the track so quickly, but I imagined him leaping over the railing and running to me when he saw I was hurt. My coach set me down next to my dad. "She probably pulled her hamstring muscle," coach said.

I heard the sympathy in Dad's voice, "Yeah, she probably did." He put his arm around me and helped me off the track. "I'm so sorry, sugar."

I choked back my tears and said, "It hurts, Dad."

"I know, sugar, I know."

We made our way to the car, and Dad helped me inside. As soon as the car door shut, the tears streamed down my face. Not only was I hurt and disappointed, but I was angry with myself for ignoring the pain I felt in my leg during warmups. I felt so stupid. I cried, "I can't believe this happened. Why did I have to fall right before the finish line? I think I was in first place."

"I know. I saw you. You did great."

For a few minutes we drove home quietly until Dad broke the silence.

"Did you hear me cheering for you?"

"No."

"I was cheering for you pretty loud."

"I don't know. I don't think I heard you." I envisioned Dad cheering in the stands. I had grown accustomed to Dad's zeal for sporting events and figured he was probably the loudest one out there. It was nice to know that Dad was that enthusiastic about my race.

Dad laughed nervously and looked over at me. "I screamed, 'Run for Daddy'!"

"You said that? Run for Daddy? Really loud?" I asked, hoping I had heard him wrong.

"Yeah, it just came out when I was cheering for you. Run for Daddy!"

I suddenly saw my entire eighth-grade existence flashing before my eyes. I pictured the other parents in the stands looking over at my dad when they heard him shout, "Run for Daddy!" at the top of his lungs. I prayed none of my teammates heard, and if they did, I hoped they didn't know whose dad he was. Worse yet, I pictured myself walking the hallways while kids laughed and pointed their fingers, "There goes the daddy's girl. Run for Daddy!"

What on earth would provoke him to shout that? I hadn't called him "Daddy" in at least two or three years by my count. *Couldn't he just cheer like a normal parent?*

I repeated it over and over in my head, "Run for Daddy. Run for Daddy." And I slowly came to a realization. Dad wasn't just in the stands observing the race. He was cheering me on so wildly, so passionately, that he lost himself for a moment. Dad was cheering me on this time as if to say, "See that girl out in front with the scrawny legs? That's my daughter!" Watching me run turned him into a crazed fan. I guess that was pretty cool. Maybe it wasn't so bad to have a dad who couldn't cheer like a "normal" parent.

Over the next few weeks, I couldn't help but laugh to myself when I thought about what Dad had done. It somehow lessened the pain and discouragement to know that he was so proud of me as he watched me race that night.

I've considered taking up running again for a while now. After all, I'm thirty-five, about the age Dad was when he took up the sport. I could certainly use the exercise, and it would eliminate the guilt I feel when I fill out that annoying questionnaire at the doctor's office. "Do you exercise regularly?"

"Yes, sometimes," I hesitantly write, figuring doing laundry and dancing to Wiggles videos should count for something. Health benefits and a clear conscience aside, when I think about running, my greatest motivation is that it would make Dad proud. He would still be my biggest fan. Because I know that at thirteen or thirty-five, whether I'm running, or writing, or just raising my kids, Dad will be on the sidelines enthusiastically cheering me on. "Run for Daddy! Run for Daddy!"

✝ The Pastor Says . . .

Every time I raced I got a prize, but not the kind of prize you're probably thinking of. Yes, I won and placed in some races, for which I got some medals, but the real prize I received after every race was delivered by my dad.

Like Tammy's dad, my dad was at almost all of my track meets, cheering for me, holding my gym bag, and delivering my prize after I finished. I have asthma, and I don't know why, but breathing fast for an extended time would cause me to get sick after every single race. It happened so much that my coach wanted to design a shirt that I could wear to every race that would read "Coach O'Brien Makes Me Sick."

Typically, dads aren't allowed on the infield. It would kind of be like having a dad in the locker room or dugout, but my dad somehow finagled a way to get himself at my side after every race, while I regurgitated in the infield just past the finish line.

He had to be at my side. That's the only way he could deliver my prize: his love in the form of a hug and an "I love you."

Great prize, huh? I knew you'd think so. It was a great prize because it would never tarnish, break, or get lost. My dad's love was eternal. No one could ever take it away from me. I loved it. I looked forward to it. I ran for it. Dad's love and approval were worth every practice, every sprain, every blister, every bead of sweat, every Coach O'Brien joke, and every training mile.

We're in a race, too. That's Paul's message to a group of runners (aka Christians) in Corinth. Corinth was famous for being the host of an Olympic-type event called the Isthmean Games, so the Christians in Corinth were familiar with athletes, races, and prizes. The athletes who competed in the Isthmean Games—and won—received several prizes. Immediately after an athlete won his event, his name, his father's name, and the name of the city where he was born would be announced to the crowd. As soon as possible, an original song was written and performed in his honor. This song would be sung during all of the celebratory events. The night after the victory, a feast would be thrown in the victor's honor. At this event the athlete would be given what they considered to be the most valuable prize: a wreath. The victor's wreath was made from an olive tree and was displayed prominently until it was placed on the victor's head. All that training, all that work, for a piece of olive tree that would turn brown and eventually crumble to pieces in your hand.

Doesn't seem to make sense, does it? To work so hard and so long for something that doesn't last. That's why Paul wrote, "Everyone who competes in the games goes into strict training. They do it to get a crown that will not last; but we do it to get a crown that will last forever."

Paul reminds us that at the end of this race (aka this life), as we're exhaling for the last time, God will come to our side—just past the finish line—and give us our prize, but it's not the kind of prize that most people would probably think of. It's an eternal crown. It's a great prize because it will never tarnish, break, or get lost. It's going to be worth every struggle, every tear, and every moment of faithfulness.

Great prize, huh? That's why I'm running for Daddy.

—Arron Chambers

Spiritual Lessons in Action

List the things you are looking forward to most about Heaven. This is why you are running this race called life. Now, list your favorite things about the Lord and remember that this is who is going to be waiting for us when we finish the race.

Standing in the Presence of the Almighty

By Robin Sigars

He gives strength to the weary and increases the power of the weak. Even youths grow tired and weary, and young men stumble and fall; but those who hope in the LORD will renew their strength. They will soar on wings like eagles; they will run and not grow weary, they will walk and not be faint.

——ISAIAH 40:29–31

It had been an incredibly stressful week. It was the week my wife, Diann, was diagnosed with cancer. Five months earlier she had given birth to our fifth child, Collin, and since his birth she had been experiencing complications.

On December 29, 1992, Diann went in for a simple procedure that would either help her heal or confirm that she did, in fact, have cancer. After the procedure started, it was obvious to the doctors that Diann had cancer, and it looked far worse than we could have imagined. Phone calls were immediately made, and miraculously she was admitted for exploratory surgery in five days at Kansas University Medical Center.

Our trip to Kansas City was very stressful; we hardly spoke because we were both so afraid. Time seemed to stand still and yet go by so fast.

We met with the doctor, and he shared with us that Diann's cancer was pretty serious. We went back to our motel room for the evening, and we simply held each other and cried for what seemed like hours. We knelt next to the bed and we prayed for a miracle, we prayed for our five children, and we prayed for the power and courage to face whatever would come our way. Neither of us realized that the storm had only begun, but that God would truly use us and make a difference in our lives.

The next morning's surgery came very early. As I sat in the waiting room, I fidgeted, tried to read old magazines, watched all the other people visiting family and friends, and walked around the hospital. Time went on and on, and I began to suspect that things weren't going well and that I was going to be hit once again with bad news.

Finally, the doctor came and got me. We walked silently to a small consultation room, the last one on the left. The room was very simple, with a desk and X-ray light. The doctor sat down, sighed, and began to talk to me very slowly to be sure that I didn't miss anything that he was saying, but, really, I was lost after his first statement.

"Mr. Sigars, it's worse than we thought. Diann is full of cancer."

He began sharing all the things that he and his staff were going to do to my wife, but my head was swimming with hurt, anger, and loss. He said, "Mr. Sigars, you've got to prepare yourself and your family for one of three things that will happen to your wife over the next six months. First of all, within the next six months, your wife is going to die of cancer. You've got to prepare yourself and your family for that. Or, in the next six months your wife will be healed of cancer."

Then very sternly, very precisely, he looked at me and said, "You've got to understand that in the next six months with all the treatments, all the radical things we are going to do, the third possibility is that I and my staff personally could kill your wife. You've got to prepare yourself for that."

I had to make myself breathe, I had to focus my mind, my heart was racing and I couldn't seem to focus my sight. My wife, the mother of my children, was probably going to die. He continued talking about what was going to happen next, all the setup stuff, the chemo treatments and radiation. Finally, he put his hands on the desk, pushed himself away from the desk, and looked at me for a moment before he said his next words. "Robin, I don't see any hope for Diann."

No hope! No chance! That's what he was telling me about my wife. She was going to die!

As he walked out of that office, he left me there all alone. I was mad at God. I looked up to the ceiling of that small room and I began to cry out to God. I must admit to you that I wasn't a great example at that time. I told Him that I hated Him. I asked Him how was I going to continue working for Christ In Youth, how was I going to continue traveling to churches and conventions speaking to teens, how in the world was I ever going to raise five children, especially a little boy who would never know his mother. I finally took my fist and looked up at the ceiling and made a promise to never serve Him again.

We spent the next four days trying to get Diann well enough to make the trip back home. I never shared with Diann what the doctor had said about her cancer. I simply kept it and my anger to myself. I didn't want to share with her that I wasn't going to do anything for God ever again. Tests were run. Di was mapped for radiation, and appointments were made for us to come back up to Kansas City.

On Sunday, Diann was released and I made the phone calls for someone to come up to Kansas City and get us. As we were waiting, it hit her that we were going to miss communion with our home church, so she thought that maybe we should do communion there in the hospital together.

I was mad at God and certainly didn't want to do a communion service with just my wife and myself. That would be way too intimate for me right now. I looked at her and said, "We can't do communion; we're in a hospital."

She looked at me as only a wife can do, especially a wife married to a minister, and said, "We're going to do communion!"

I went to the nurse's station right across from Diann's room. The nurses had become very impressed with Diann already, with her strength and faith in God. So once I asked for some grape juice and a muffin, they knew exactly what we wanted. I went back to the room and put the little meal tray in front of Diann and opened the can of grape juice. I poured her a small amount like communion at church, but for myself, I poured a whole cup of communion. Diann looked at me with wonder at what I was doing. I told her, "I'm tired of getting a little bit of grape juice for communion; I want a whole cup since I'm the one pouring the juice this morning." In reality, I was serving Diann communion, but for me, I was simply having a muffin with some grape juice to drink.

Once again she looked at me, and I knew I was in trouble. I was playing in my mind what I was going to do when she wanted me to pray for the communion. I didn't want to talk with God. I hated God right then.

But she made the matter worse. She looked at me and said, "Robin, we need to sing."

"Sing!" I shot back, "We can't sing; this is a hospital. People can't sing in a hospital."

Once again I got that look. "Robin, we sing in a hospital all the time."

Then she did it. She looked deep into my eyes, "We're going to sing!"

I can't tell you all the songs that we sang, but since that day, I have prayed that God would never let me forget the last song we sang. It was a simple little chorus entitled, "I will not be ashamed of you, Father."

We sang it over and over again. And when we were done, I knew that I would serve God again. I knew that He would be in control of my life and the outcome of Diann's, no matter what.

I finally prayed and asked God to forgive me and to take my life, to take our lives, and use them for His kingdom. I prayed for the emblems of communion, we took them, and then, as Diann lay back down on the bed, I moved away and leaned against the wall to regain some composure from the moment.

As I moved back, I saw them. I saw two nurses standing there in the doorway, hand in hand, tears running down their faces. And at that moment I realized I was standing in the midst of the Almighty

God. Not because of me or my faith, but because in the darkest moment of life a woman of faith said that she would serve God, and nothing—not even the darkness of death—would stop her.

Diann did get better and fought her battle for three years. On October 28, 1995, with her five children around her, she told each one good-bye, and then went home to be with Jesus.

✝ *The Pastor Says . . .*

Today, I want to tell you about Etty Hillesum. Etty Hillesum's life and death have always inspired me.

Etty, a young Jewish woman from Amsterdam, documented the last two years of her life in a diary she kept while enduring Nazi persecution. During this terrible time, while living in a concentration camp in Holland called Westbrook, when all that could be seen in every direction was death, Etty somehow managed to see hope. Her diaries were published after her death in a book entitled *An Interrupted Life: The Diaries of Etty Hillesum, 1941–1943* (New York: Pantheon, 1983). In her diaries, we see a young woman with a mature faith.

On September 7, 1943, Etty and her family were moved from Westbrook to another concentration camp. They were loaded onto a train and sent to Auschwitz. As they were pulling out, Etty tossed a card out the train window—a card on which she had documented the facts and defined her outlook on life: "We left the camp singing."

She died two months later at the age of twenty-nine.

Diann Sigars's life and death inspire me, too. Hope is inspirational. Not just hope in general. Some hope is not inspirational, at all. In fact, some hope is empty—vain. Like hoping to pass a test without studying, or hoping to get a promotion without working, or hoping to have a great marriage without sacrificing, or hoping to win without training, or hoping to have success without planning, or hoping to not have to work at a fast-food restaurant upon retirement without saving.

I want the kind of hope that will hold my heart until the very last beat. Isaiah promises that "those who hope in the Lord" will find renewed strength that will help them to soar like an eagle, run without getting tired, and walk without fainting.

That's real hope. That's the kind of hope that births a song in the hearts of dying women from Poland to Missouri. If I had been standing at the door with those two nurses, watching as Robin and Diann sang praise to God in the face of certain death, I know I would have cried, too.

I want that kind of hope. I want to leave singing, too.

—Arron Chambers

Spiritual Lessons in Action

Sing a song. Don't laugh! I'm serious. Promise me that you will sing a song sometime today because of the hope you have in God. Don't worry about the sound of your voice. Don't worry about who might hear you. You can sing on your way to work, or as you work around the house, or while you're in the shower. Just sing . . . and promise me that you'll do all you can to leave this life singing.

Milt's Gift

By Kimberly Ripley

You, my brothers, were called to be free. But do not use your freedom to indulge the sinful nature; rather, serve one another in love. The entire law is summed up in a single command: "Love your neighbor as yourself."

—GALATIANS 5:13,14

It was Christmas Eve 2004, and nothing seemed right in my world. Yes, I had my family and friends to be grateful for—and indeed I was. I was feeling melancholy, I guess. I didn't like feeling blue at Christmas.

I knew God's grace and mercy had been granted to our family, and I felt guilty for not accepting these gifts with joy. My mood was also hampered by what I call rites of passage. It was the first year my older two children and their prospective fiancés hadn't attended church with us on Christmas Eve. For years we'd all gone to our church's candlelight service together as a family. Some years included guests. Some years included a boyfriend or girlfriend who was long since forgotten by the following year, but for that one night they shared a special bond with our family. Now parts of our own family were missing. Had I done something wrong in raising my children? They were brought up believing that Jesus was the reason for Christmas, and that without this miracle birth from above there would be no peace on earth, goodwill toward men. Why hadn't they come to church with their family? It was simply beyond my understanding.

The service was a beautiful one—as it is each year. Carols resounded throughout the warm, inviting church, and candles lit the sanctuary, as well as the hearts of all attending. Our pastor's words enhanced the magic of that special night. Still, something felt out of place. I couldn't figure out exactly what it was. For a few years in a row, our family had significantly cut down the expense of buying presents. Oh sure, we still bought gifts for everyone, but they weren't nearly as extravagant or abundant as they'd been in previous years. Instead we spent the money on getting together as a family and on buying gifts for families in need. It should have created more of a warm, fuzzy feeling, but I really wasn't feeling very warm or fuzzy at all.

At the end of the service, a fellow church member approached me and asked what we were doing immediately following church. "Not much," I muttered, sort of distractedly.

"Can you help get Milt into bed tonight?" Louis asked. "It's my night to do it, but by the time I close up the church and get over there it's going to be pretty late. Your older boy and your husband could get him into bed, right?"

"Sure they can," I said.

Louis did a lot for our church and for its members. Milt was a longtime member who had been diagnosed with ALS, also known as Lou Gehrig's disease. Now bent and immobile, he was confined to a wheelchair throughout the day. Most nights he had the care of a male nurse to help maneuver him into bed; however, the nurse was in another state visiting his own family for Christmas. Louis had been helping Milt's wife, Dolly, each night that the nurse was away. Certainly we could do this one simple favor on Christmas Eve.

My husband made arrangements with Dolly at the church, telling her we'd arrive at their home in just a few minutes. Our older boy is our twenty-year-old son, Jim. A big, strong young man, we knew that between him and my husband, Milt would be safely transferred between wheelchair and bed.

A couple of friends got wind of our Christmas Eve errand. "I can take Elizabeth and Jonathan with me," one offered. Elizabeth and Jonathan were our children, thirteen and eleven at the time.

"You don't want them over there seeing Milt like that on Christmas Eve," another well-meaning parishioner added. Sure we did. And why not? Not a family who sheltered or minced words with our children, we saw no reason to keep Milt's condition from the kids. They'd known him from church their whole lives and had seen his decline from walking, to using a walker, to not coming to church any more at all. This was reality. People get sick. They suffer. We had no intention of sheltering our children from that fact.

Thanking our concerned friends, we bid them goodnight. After sharing warm Christmas greetings with our pastor, his wife, and many of our friends, we piled everyone in the car for the short drive to Milt and Dolly's house. On the way we explained to our younger kids that Milt's health had failed. Our older boy seemed concerned about his ability to be of use, and we assured him that Milt and Dolly would explain the process. All we needed to contribute were strong arms and some compassion.

Dolly greeted us at the door with gratitude and warm Christmas greetings, and led us to Milt in a room off their kitchen. Milt sat, bent and twisted, in his wheelchair, but turned his head as far as he could in our direction and wished us a merry Christmas. Within seconds, it was easy to see that Milt was still Milt. His sense of humor was fully intact, as was his knowledge of current events and local happenings. He quickly explained to Rip (my husband) and Jim how to operate the lift that would smoothly transfer him from his wheelchair to his bed, just a few short feet away. Dolly assisted with instructions. Rip and Jim carefully moved him into bed. I chattered on about the numerous books I saw lying around.

"Do you still read a lot, Milt?" I asked.

"Oh, yes."

Dolly smiled. "He reads a lot of biographies," she said.

The next few minutes were spent acquiring a recommended list of reading from Milt. Some of our reading interests were similar. Rip and Jim continued getting him settled for the night.

"Take these pants off," Milt directed gently. "Don't worry, I have underpants on." Everyone laughed. "Now put this pillow under my head," he said. Another pillow pushed against his feet to keep him from rubbing on the footboard of the hospital bed.

Rip and Milt engaged in a conversation about boating. A long-time lover of the sea, Milt had sailed for fun and was a member of the Power Squadron, a civilian's group known for helping the Coast Guard teach boating education. Dolly offered Christmas cookies all around. We turned down offers of coffee and cold drinks. Little did we know the true gift that would be ours that Christmas Eve.

The evening ended with well wishes, words of Christmas cheer, and an offer on our behalf to sit with Milt if Dolly needed to get out of the house. Sadly, that never came to fruition. Milt passed away just a few weeks after Christmas. Our family was away on vacation at the time.

When we returned, it occurred to me just what a precious Christmas gift we'd been given by Milt and Dolly on Christmas Eve. Milt had allowed us a glimpse at true humility. We were privileged to share in his weakness and lend a helping hand. Dolly showed grace in the face of great adversity. She remained steadfast and cheerful despite their knowledge of Milt's inevitable fate. It reminded me of the people in that first Christmas story—a humble beginning for a mighty man, and the grace of His mother as she watched His blessed sacrifice. I knew with certainty we'd been blessed.

Next Christmas Eve we'll attend church services as usual, but I know I'll arrive with a lighter feeling in my heart. I'll be grateful for my family, despite the number of them joining us in the pew. I'll sing the Lord's praises and add a special thank-you for a very special Christmas gift received the year before. And I know many others will do just the same. My husband, my younger children, Jim, and most of all, Dolly, will each in our own way raise our eyes and hearts toward heaven and say thank you for Milt's gift—one he never even realized he was giving. We'll say a thank you to Louis, too. For what he thought might be inconvenient had instead wound up a cherished Christmas memory.

✝ *The Pastor Says* . . .

When I stop and think about it, I realize that I can be pretty self-indulgent. In a typical day I will look at myself in the mirror about forty-six times; position myself in the fastest lane, shortest line, and longest buffet; feel sorry for myself; and talk to myself incessantly. It is the atypical day on which I don't think about myself.

Christmas should be an atypical day. The day we set aside to remember that God loved us so much that He sent his son to this smelly, dirty, and ordinary place to save us from ourselves and our sin is a day we need to set aside our selfishness. But, just the opposite happens—at least when we're children. When I was a child, I couldn't sleep on Christmas Eve as I anticipated all of the wonderful gifts that Santa was bringing for me. Me.

I wasn't thinking of anybody but me and all of the presents that I was going to receive. I was selfish. Selfishness is a sign of immaturity.

My two-year-old daughter thinks the world revolves around her, and in some respects, she's right. She cries—and I come. She falls—and I drop everything to pick her up. She's hungry—and I feed her. She's dirty—and her mom changes her (you don't think I'm completely selfless, do you?).

I hope my daughter gets over this, and I expect she will. It's fine—even expected—now, but self-centeredness is no longer cute when it looks like an adult. I expect my daughter to look for "Milts" at Christmas time—people in need.

Mature Christians understand the importance of serving others on both typical and atypical days. As the Apostle Paul points out, we are free and we can do whatever we want, but we should want to "serve one another in love." Selflessness is a sign of maturity.

"Milts" are everywhere. They are working down the hall from you. They live in the apartment downstairs. They sold you gas and a pack of gum this morning. They are sitting in the hall at the local nursing home. They live next door and they are living under the bridge. They are even sitting three rows in front of you in church. Mature people will put down the mirror to see that people in need are all around us.

I don't know when you're reading this, I do know that Christmas can't be more than twelve months away. I can't wait for Christmas. I'm already thinking about what I want for Christmas.

Do you know what I want for Christmas? Whatever Milt wants.

—Arron Chambers

Spiritual Lessons in Action

Buy a Christmas gift for a "Milt" in your life, wrap the gift in Christmas paper, and give it to him or her as soon as you have the opportunity.

A Place for Walt

By C. Robert Wetzel

Now the body is not made up of one part but of many. If the foot should say, "Because I am not a hand, I do not belong to the body," it would not for that reason cease to be part of the body. And if the ear should say, "Because I am not an eye, I do not belong to the body," it would not for that reason cease to be part of the body. If the whole body were an eye, where would the sense of hearing be? If the whole body were an ear, where would the sense of smell be? But in fact God has arranged the parts in the body, every one of them, just as he wanted them to be. If they were all one part, where would the body be? As it is, there are many parts, but one body. If one part suffers, every part suffers with it; if one part is honored, every part rejoices with it.

—I CORINTHIANS 17:14–20, 26

Walt was in his seventies, but he had the mind of an eight-year-old, or younger. The story was that when he was eight years old, his head was run over by a farm wagon. He barely survived the accident, but his mental growth never developed. As I remember, he lived with a sister some two or three miles from the small Oklahoma church where I served fifty years ago. Every Sunday morning he walked the distance to be at services. Sometimes he would be given a ride, but usually he was on the road so early he was the first to arrive at the church building.

There was nothing wrong with Walt's appetite. He always carried a fork and spoon in the top of his bib overalls just in case the church might be having a fellowship dinner. He was always accompanied by his dog, named Pard, that followed him into church and curled up under his chair. By and large, Pard was content to sleep through the entire service, and probably was not the only one of God's creatures who slept through my sermons. It was said that Walt had been baptized as a boy, but whether he had been or not, he was very much a part of the church family. No one would have thought of objecting to the presence of Pard under his chair during services, nor would they have ever thought to curtail Walt's voracious appetite at church dinners.

The little church had found, over the years, that the only way they could get a big-name evangelist to come to the church was to hold their revival meetings in August. This was an Oklahoma August, before air conditioning. Larger churches would not have considered trying to have a revival meeting at the hottest and most humid time of the year. But evangelists whose livelihood depended upon a full schedule of revival meetings had to take what they could get in August. And we got one of the best that year.

On a Saturday night, the evangelist and his wife arrived in town with their house trailer. It was arranged for them to park the trailer immediately adjoining the church annex so that they could connect to electricity and water. This done, they settled down for a good night's sleep in preparation for the busy two weeks ahead of them.

The next morning Walt arrived earlier than usual. He was fascinated by the trailer. He went into the annex and took a chair at a window where he could see the trailer. Not only could he see it, but also his window was opposite the bedroom window of the evangelist and his wife. I do not know which one awoke first that morning, but when they looked out their bedroom window, they saw the face of this whiskery old man smiling at them, not two feet away!

This unfortunate beginning of their acquaintance did not get better when an incident occurred during the communion service later that morning. Being August, all of the windows and doors were left wide open. There was hardly a problem with traffic noise on Sunday morning in this small town of 400. The pianist was playing a hymn as the communion emblems were being passed. Pard slept quietly under his master's chair. But then some people rode by on horseback, and we discovered that Pard had a particular dislike for horses. He began barking and tried to go for the horses. In his excitement, he found himself trapped by the rungs of the chair. And thus all he could do was bark furiously and run in place underneath the chair, paws scratching loudly on the rough wood floor. Eventually Walt stood up and raised the chair. Pard made his escape and went running down the street after the horses. The pianist never missed a note, but I am afraid our evangelist was chagrined.

When Pard disrupted the communion service, our people smiled as they would have if a young couple's baby had suddenly begun crying. After all, Walt was Walt, he was our Walt, and there was a place for him in this community of believers.

Most every congregation I have served has had its Walt. They were not always old men whose mental growth had stopped somewhere in childhood. Sometimes they were just decidedly different. "One sandwich short of a picnic," as the English expression goes. Sometimes they were troublesome, but most of the time they were just another part of that amazing collage of inadequate, individualistic, saved-by-grace people that we call the church. Walt may not have made the best impression on our evangelist that hot summer day in Oklahoma, but he was never the problem of a James and a John vying for a preferential position on either side of Jesus. Walt was still the little child who somehow was attracted to and found acceptance in the Body of Christ.

With whatever problems this small Oklahoma congregation had, not least of which was being served by an eighteen-year-old Bible college student, everyone understood their ministry to Walt. He was, in his seventieth year, still a child who, for reasons we did not understand, walked several miles every Sunday to be with the people of God, whether we had a fellowship dinner or not. Just as I am not inclined to speculate as to why little children are drawn to Jesus, I do not offer any explanation for Walt. Perhaps I can have a good talk with him when I catch up with him in Heaven. In the meantime, I can only thank God for what my first congregation taught me as to what it means to be a part of the Body of Christ. There was a place for Walt.

✝ *The Pastor Says . . .*

I want to talk to you about your pinkie toe—actually, my wife's pinkie toe.

My wife has a habit of breaking her pinkie toe. It seems that about every two years, my wife will kick her foot on the bed, on a toy, on a curb, or on something else that she didn't see, and break her toe. I always know when she's done it. It always starts with a loud banging noise, followed by my wife's reaction. Now, my wife was raised with three brothers in the mountains of Upper East Tennessee, so—if she were so inclined—she could swear for about three minutes without repeating herself, but—since she's not so inclined—she just groans. I always feel so bad that she feels so bad.

I've never broken my little toe, but I know it hurts because I've seen what it does to my wife. When she breaks her pinkie toe, she can't walk. It hurts to put even the smallest amount of weight on her foot, so, for a couple of days, she has to hop around on one leg if she wants to get around. It hurts to put on a sock, and a shoe feels like an instrument of torture.

My wife does not need to be convinced that her pinkie toe is important. It may be a small part of the body, but it is definitely an important part of the body.

Every part of the body is important. The Church is a body, and every part of the Church is important.

Apparently, some of the members of the church in Corinth were not convinced that some of the other members were an important part of their church, so the Apostle Paul reminded them that every single part of the body, although different, is important. He also reminded them that, in a healthy body, the parts share both pain and joy.

In a healthy church, there's a place for the mouths—those who speak words of inspiration, healing, and encouragement.

In a healthy church, there's a place for the hands—those who touch the hurting, serve the needy, and point the way to God.

In a healthy church, there's a place for the arms—those who hold the tired, protect the vulnerable, and lift the downcast.

In a healthy church, there's a place for the legs—those who stand up for truth and righteousness.

In a healthy church, there's a place for the feet—those who take the message of hope and salvation to everyone everywhere.

In a healthy church body, there's a place for every part, because every part of the body is important.

In a healthy church body, there's even a place for pinkie toes like me and Walt.

—Arron Chambers

Spiritual Lessons in Action

Take a few moments and write a note of encouragement, make a phone call, or send an e-mail to a couple of the "Walts" in your life to let them know how special they are to you.

Mercy

By Tamela Hancock Murray

Jesus went through all the towns and villages, teaching in their synagogues, preaching the good news of the kingdom and healing every disease and sickness. When he saw the crowds, he had compassion on them, because they were harassed and helpless, like sheep without a shepherd. Then he said to his disciples, "The harvest is plentiful but the workers are few. Ask the Lord of the harvest, therefore, to send out workers into his harvest field."

—MATTHEW 9:35–38

I was a tweener before that tender age between childhood and thirteen became a major deal to marketers. What I remember most is not how much I influenced my parents' spending—which seemed to me to be not at all—but how I often found myself to be more ambitious in spirit than action. This applied especially to farm work.

My grandparents operated an independent farm four miles from where I lived with my parents in our small southern Virginia town, so I was a frequent visitor. I wanted to contribute, so Grandpa let me stock daily feed in the nine cows' individual troughs. Successful in this minimal effort consuming all of ten minutes, I felt certain I was ready for a more significant assignment. I begged to milk the cows, but my grandpa and Uncle Eldridge were both afraid I'd suffer a kick if I yanked too hard. So my pleading went unheeded.

Hope arose anew when, one steaming summer afternoon, Uncle Eldridge said he planned to chop tobacco. "What does that mean?" I asked.

"That's when you take a hoe and clear the weeds from between the tobacco seedlings," he explained.

"Why do you do that?"

"So the weeds won't choke the plants, and they can grow." Eldridge crossed his arms, tanned to a deep shade of burnt sienna. From underneath the short sleeves of his white T-shirt, his biceps bulged with enough vigor to tempt a professional wrestler to challenge him to a match. Every once in a while, Uncle Eldridge would let me hit his biceps as hard as I could, once or twice. They felt like living rocks. No matter how hard I hit, he didn't flinch. I didn't know enough about health to appreciate the fact that despite such developed arms, the rest of him remained lean. I raised my own bicep and managed to summon a half-inch bulge. Although I didn't aspire to arms as large as my uncle's, I thought that chopping tobacco that afternoon would set me off to a good start at becoming stronger.

"Can I help? Please?"

He cast me a doubtful look, but after some verbal wrangling and amused permission from my grandmother, he allowed me to go along with him. He fetched two hoes from the shed and handed me one.

"I have to carry this myself?"

He nodded.

This was not getting off to a good start.

By the time we walked to the field, I was already hotter than I remembered being in a long time, even though central air conditioning was not yet available to us, and I had not become spoiled by such luxury. Though Uncle Eldridge had wisely waited until an hour or so before suppertime to begin the chore to avoid the harshest rays of the sun, the heat from the late afternoon felt brutal on my tender, refrigerator-white skin.

We stood at the end of the field. Rows and rows of tobacco plants awaited rescue with the aid of our hoes. I viewed the horizon ahead and didn't see an end to the plants. I surveyed the side and barely discerned the other end of the field, where lush green forest prevailed.

"Which row do you want to take?" Uncle Eldridge asked.

All of them looked equally challenging to me, but I was sure I could tackle whichever one I chose. "I'll start here," I said.

"Let me show you what to do." He pointed to the tallest green plant amid other, greener plants. "See that tobacco plant? You want to be careful not to damage that. You just want to get rid of the weeds in between. Like this." With ten swift and deep strokes, he dug into the dirt and cleaned around five plants.

"Oh. OK." I smiled and nodded, trying not to show how impatient I was becoming. Why was he chopping all the tobacco? At the rate he was progressing, none of the work would be left for me!

Finally, I watched as my uncle took the next row and chopped. And chopped. And chopped. He seemed to move so fast I thought he would win a prize if he had been in a race.

Now it was my turn. With gusto, I threw the blade of my hoe into the ground, being careful. Instead of the dirt giving way like water, as it seemed to for Uncle Eldridge, the clump of turf resisted. Offending weeds moved only about an inch, rather than the foot they had yielded from the powerful whack of my uncle's hoe. I tried again, harder this time. A few weeds surrendered, but more mocked me. With one hit, my uncle could accomplish more than I could in five. With great effort, I cleared the dirt around two plants.

I stopped and leaned against my hoe, peering at the sun. Why was it so hot? "Uncle Eldridge?" I shouted to him.

"What is it?"

"Do you have any water?" I was hoping for a mayonnaise jar filled with cool well water. Even lukewarm well water would have been welcome at that point.

"No."

What? No water? No refreshment to help us through such a tiring chore? "I'm thirsty. Can I go back to the house and get a glass of water?" My determination to secure refreshment overrode my remembrance that the trip to the field had taken a good fifteen minutes.

"No."

What? No? What did he mean, no? How could my uncle, usually the image of kindness, be so cruel? Clearly the sun had gotten to him, too. "Please?"

"No."

"But I'm thirsty!" The more I spoke, the drier my throat felt. "What am I supposed to do?"

"Just concentrate on the breeze. Enjoy that, and let it cool you."

Now I was sure that the sun had fried a big hole right through his skull and sizzled away the part of his brain that registered temperature. Had I been near a phone, I might have summoned the local volunteer rescue squad—after I drank a glass of water.

Nevertheless, I tried. Imitating his example, I set my own face against the air and watched for the leaves on the trees to move. Maybe God would send a breeze strong enough to make the pine trees sway, even. I sent up a hopeful prayer.

A few seconds later, God answered with the gentlest puff of air I've ever witnessed. And while I was happy for any assistance, the moving gust was too hot to offer much relief, at least not from my perspective.

"It's not helping." I saw his progress and figured he deserved to call it a day. "Can't we go back?" I looked at the house with the most yearning expression I could muster.

"Not yet."

"But I want some water."

"By not being able to get a glass of water whenever you feel like it, you will learn to appreciate it."

"I do," I promised.

"Now you will appreciate it even more."

I sighed. Knowing well our family's stubborn streak, I sensed the time had come to give up on reasoning with him. I would have to keep chopping. I gave the weeds two more whacks. Three scrawny weeds submitted to the grim reaper.

"Can I get some water after I finish this row?" I asked.

By this time he had started on the next row. Or maybe it was a third row. He regarded my lack of progress and nevertheless consented.

Invigorated by the thought, I cleared the weeds around three more plants. Progress seemed sweet until I looked back up the row and realized the end was nowhere near. Aching shoulders joined relentless thirst. I looked at the beckoning trees.

Embarrassment swept over me. I had started out with such good intentions, determined to chop at least as many rows as Uncle Eldridge, or at least to make a reasonably good show of work. But it was not to be. By this point I realized that if I could chop one row, victory would be mine. First, I needed a respite. I thought to myself, *If I can just get into the shade a few minutes, I'll feel better. Then I'll come back and finish this row real quick. Once I rest, it won't seem hard at all.*

"Uncle Eldridge, I'm going to sit in the shade a while and then come back and finish this row," I declared with all sincerity.

"All right."

I set down the hoe and headed for the trees. I found a grassy spot underneath a few tall pines. Seeking coolness, I lay down. The grass felt refreshing against my bare legs and arms.

As my uncle approached the end of yet another row, I could hear the sound of his hoe digging with relentless strength into the soil. I imagined the terror of the weeds, helpless against the sharp blade, and the thankfulness of the tender plants that would now thrive. I thought, *I'll shut my eyes for just a few minutes.*

The next thing I knew, my uncle was calling me. I jumped to my feet and ran to my row. It was clean. He had finished his work and mine as well. I didn't want to admit it, but I was too relieved to feel anything but gratitude.

✝ *The Pastor Says . . .*

Farming makes me tired. I've never actually lived on a farm, or actually farmed, but, like Tamela, I've seen a lot of farmers at work—and just watching farmers work makes me tired. My dad grew up on a farm, so I'm familiar with the amount of work it takes to maintain a farm and produce a harvest. My dad did more before 5:00 A.M. than most people do all day.

Farmers must not be human, because all of the humans I know have to sleep every once in a while, but farmers don't seem to need any sleep. I respect farmers so much, and I'm grateful for their work.

My dad never outgrew the work ethic that my grandfather ingrained in him. This made Saturday mornings really fun around my house when I was a teenager.

On more than a few Saturday mornings, about 7:00 A.M., when most humans (especially teens) are still sleeping, my dad would bang on my window and ask, "You gonna sleep all day?"

All day! It's 7:00 A.M. The day hasn't even started yet!, I would think to myself, but never verbalize, because I wanted to live till 8:00.

By 7:00 A.M., Dad had already finished a couple of hours of work. He was a busy man and he knew the importance of getting your work done while you still could. He used to say, "You have to make hay while the sun's still shining." He was right. He still is.

Jesus has work for us to do, too. In this passage we find Jesus working—He's probably been at it for a couple of hours— teaching, preaching, and healing. There was plenty of work to do, and he wanted to "make some hay." He saw the crowds, had compassion on them, and realized that there was work to do and He could use some help, so He knocked on the Disciples' window.

It's as if He wanted to ask them, "You gonna sleep all day?" Jesus' heart broke for hurting people, and He was willing to do anything and everything to help them find healing. He saw too many hurting people and too few workers who could help Him bring them in.

That's what farmers call it—the harvesting process—they call it "bringing in the harvest." Jesus is counting on us to help Him.

We must not miss this opportunity to join Him in the fields. If we do, we'll regret it forever.

He's knocking on the window. Can you hear Him calling? Are we going to sleep all day?

—Arron Chambers

Spiritual Lessons in Action

Set your alarm to go off five minutes from now. After setting the alarm, begin praying that God will use you today to be a blessing. When the alarm sounds, turn it off, and get to work.

The Egg Basket

By David Faust

F or God so loved the world that he gave his one and only Son, that whoever believes in him shall not perish but have eternal life."

—JOHN 3:16

There was a chicken house on the farm where I grew up. Like my older brothers, I did my daily chores every morning before breakfast: tossing corn to the hogs, feeding hay to the cows, and the like.

One of my jobs was to gather the eggs each evening. I placed them carefully into a big basket made from thick wire coated with yellow plastic. I made sure the chickens had water, ground corn, and crushed oyster shells to eat.

Once in a while, I discovered an egg with a partially formed shell. In my hand these strange eggs felt soft and rubbery, like little brown balloons filled with water.

Somehow my city-slicker children managed to grow up without a chicken house nearby, but I still found chores for them to do. They washed and vacuumed the car, mowed the lawn, scrubbed the bathroom, and helped with the dishes. My grown-up daughter Michelle still hasn't forgiven me for coming up with the brilliant idea that one of her chores should be polishing my shoes every week, an idea that didn't last long.

My wife, Candy, assigned her share of household chores too, but she also was good at creating fun activities for the kids. Around Valentine's Day every year, we organized a Heart Hunt and turned our house into a hiding place for candy. The kids searched the rooms looking for hidden treasures, following silly clues we wrote on heart-shaped construction paper like "You'll find something sweet and light, under the place where you sleep at night."

On the Saturday before Easter, we conducted our own family egg hunt in the backyard. Candy and I hid colored eggs in the grass, in the flowerpots, on the picnic table, by the garden hose, and in the vee where the maple tree's limbs spread upward. It only took about five minutes for the kids to fill their baskets with eggs, and then we guided them toward the hard-to-find ones by saying, "You're getting warmer."

In late summer the tree in front of our house dropped crab apples on the grass. Barely a half-inch in diameter, these bright green fruits were hard as rocks, and sour if you dared to taste one. They were unsafe, too. The lawnmower shot them out like bullets, so I paid the kids a penny for every crab apple they collected. They tried to bargain for a higher price, but a nickel apiece seemed too pricey to me.

Growing up on a farm taught me a strong work ethic, and it sharpened my appreciation for God's creative handiwork. I hope I've passed these traits along to my children. As the years go by, I watch with pride as they honor God in their daily work. And while they no longer collect colored eggs and crab apples, I'm pretty impressed with the ideas they have collected.

In 1990, my parents decided to hold an auction and sell some of their household belongings and most of their farm equipment. The auctioneer set up tables around the lawn under the shade trees where I played softball and horseshoes as a boy.

On one table sat a familiar-looking metal basket covered with yellow plastic—the one I had used to gather eggs. I offered five dollars for it, but the price rose when an antique collector bid against me. I ended up paying $30 for it, and now I keep the egg basket in my garage above the workbench.

My mother told me later, "If I had known you wanted the egg basket, I would have given it to you for free." But I didn't mind. I learned far more than $30 worth of lessons growing up on the family farm.

✝ *The Pastor Says . . .*

It's been said that "Beauty is in the eye of the beholder." Well, I think value is, too.

You wouldn't have paid a dime for it, but she wouldn't have sold it to you for a million bucks. My daughter's favorite stuffed animal was a stuffed lion she called Simba. She got it before she was a year old and still had it nine years later. Simba was Ashton's constant companion. He ate with her, slept with her, traveled with her, watched TV with her, and comforted her when no person could. Where Ashton was, Simba was, too. Simba was dirty, tattered, and had a peculiar smell that detergent couldn't quite conquer, but none of that stopped Ashton from loving Simba.

I wonder if you know how valuable you are to God. Do you feel valuable? Do you feel loved?

You're not just loved, you're "so loved," as today's passage reminds us. Maybe you feel too dirty, tattered, or foul to love. Maybe you've made some choices that you regret. Maybe you feel defined by your weakest moment and no better than your worst mistake. Maybe you feel like your life isn't worth a dime.

God is a lot of "omni" words. He's omnipresent, which means he's everywhere at once. He's omnipotent, which means he's the most powerful being in the world. And he's omniscient, which means he knows everything.

He knew that Adam and Eve were going to eat the fruit off of the tree, but he still created a beautiful world for them. He knew that the Children of Israel were going to grumble about him in the desert, but he still created a "land flowing with milk and honey" for them. He knew that Judas would betray him with a kiss, but he still washed his feet. And he knew that you and I would sin, but he still sent his only son to die for us so that we could have the hope of eternal life.

Why? Why would God send his son to die for us—knowing good and well that we do foolish things and make irresponsible choices? Why? Because he doesn't just love us—he "so loves us."

Ashton "so loved" Simba, when we lost Simba, she began to sob. Ashton was cheering in a competition at the Arena in downtown Orlando, and she'd asked us to bring Simba. My wife put Simba in her purse, but somewhere and somehow in the mass of people and the exodus out of the Arena, we lost Simba.

I ran back to the Arena and found only locked doors and security guards. "I need to get in," I pleaded.

The security guard said, "No."

"But, my daughter's favorite stuffed animal is in here, and I have to find it."

"I'm sorry sir, but I can't let you back in."

Desperate I asked, "Do you have a daughter? I have to try to find her Simba."

The guard softened. "OK, but make it quick."

I searched and searched, but Simba was not to be found. I'll never forget the look in my daughter's eyes when I walked back empty-handed. We all wept quietly, and not a single word was spoken during the thirty-minute drive home.

Ashton "so loved" Simba and would have done anything to get him back. I "so loved" Ashton and would have done anything to get him back, too. God "so loved" us, so he let his son die on a cross to get us back from certain death.

We are valuable. God loves us like Ashton loved Simba, and like David loved that egg basket, and when you "so love" something like that, you'll do whatever it takes to get it back.

—Arron Chambers

Spiritual Lessons in Action

Remember what you cherished when you were a child. Was it a blanket? A stuffed animal? A toy? As you think about how much you loved that item, remember how much God loves you and how valuable you are to Him.

Change Through
a Manger

By Leslie Wood

While Jesus was in Bethany in the home of a man known as Simon the Leper, a woman came to him with an alabaster jar of very expensive perfume, which she poured on his head as he was reclining at the table. When the disciples saw this, they were indignant. "Why this waste?" they asked. "This perfume could have been sold at a high price and the money given to the poor." Aware of this, Jesus said to them, "Why are you bothering this woman? She has done a beautiful thing to me. The poor you will always have with you, but you will not always have me. When she poured this perfume on my body, she did it to prepare me for burial. I tell you the truth, wherever this gospel is preached throughout the world, what she has done will also be told, in memory of her."

—MATTHEW 26:6—13

Don't you just love Christmastime? All the decorations, wonderful songs, and poignant movies?

My childhood Christmas memories are filled with happy times with family and friends. I can remember riding on the church bus, caroling to our friends and neighbors. One year, we went to see *The Nutcracker* on Christmas Eve. Another year, we saw the movie *Oliver!* When I became a mom, I had dreams of creating special memories with my own children, although, the event I'm about to describe can't really be described as beautiful or special. It was just—well, just bizarre.

It was the Christmas of 2000. We had been living in Stafford, Virginia, for about four years. Our church did not have a building, so we were meeting in a middle-school gymnasium. Because we had church in a gym, it was often difficult to create those special, beautiful memories that I remember as a child.

Christmas Eve services offered a wonderful opportunity to reach out to the community and to the church family with the message of Jesus' birth. In fact, the Christmas Eve service is an easy opportunity to reach out to the community. It takes a lot to mess up a Christmas Eve service. After all, it's Christmas—right?

Well, that year we decided we would put a manger up in the front to allow our church people to participate in giving to others less fortunate. Everyone could either bring in nonperishable food items or a monetary gift to put in the manger. We envisioned a deeply meaningful time of sharing and giving—a truly wonderful memory in the making. Oh, it was a memory in the making, all right.

The evening of December 24 arrived. Earlier that day, we had gone to the Rainforest Café in northern Virginia, which had become a tradition in our family. My twins, Connor and Taylor, who were just five at the time, and my daughter Kendall, who was two, were so excited! Not only was it Jesus' birthday tonight, it also was the night a present could be opened. To add to the fun, we had my aunt and uncle from Florida visiting for the evening. They were on their way to Williamsburg and had decided to come up for our service. So, anticipating a wonderful time, we bundled the kids up and headed for the church.

As we walked in, the candles were burning and beautiful music was playing. We found a seat in the last row, because as always, we came in at the last minute. My husband, the minister, spoke and prepared our hearts for the time of giving. I wish I had been prepared. I, of course, had forgotten to bring canned goods with me, and only remembered after we sat down that I was supposed to have brought something to put in the manger. My kids, who could sense my concern, leaned over to me and asked, "Mommy, what are we going to put in the manger?" I froze in panic and started digging in my wallet and the bottom of my purse for money, which is where all my loose change always ended up. Wouldn't you know it? I had no bills with me, only change. If I had stopped to think about it, I probably would have stayed in my seat. Being the minister's wife, I knew that my absence from participating would be noticed, especially by my children, so we proceeded to make our way to the front.

Most everyone else had already put gifts in the manger, so now it was our turn. Upon approaching the manger, I looked down and realized that the manger had big open slats in the side. Too late. My two-year-old daughter enthusiastically threw her money in, and down and out it went. Before I could warn the other two, their change dropped into the manger, fell out, and proceeded to roll across the gym floor. Luckily, the beautiful song being sung drowned out the sounds of coins hitting and rolling across the basketball court. Before I could grab him, my industrious son, Connor, crawled under the manger, rescued some of the money, and said—loudly—"Mommy, I found some!" He then threw it in again and well, you know what happened.

By this time, I wanted to throw myself under the manger with my son, who was once again under the manger trying to rescue the money for Baby Jesus. I looked behind me and the entire front row was on the verge of hysterics. To the sounds of hushed laughter and "O Holy Night," I grabbed my kids and quickly walked back to our seats, which as you remember, were in the last row.

I wish that I had been prepared to give my gift. If I had just put three or four dollars in my wallet, there would have been no need to be ashamed or embarrassed about my gift. My intentions were good, but like so many times before, I hadn't given my best.

I would have preferred not to stop at our seats, but head on out the door and home, but we didn't. We sat down, grateful for God's love and his grace . . . and for His manger.

✝ *The Pastor Says* . . .

I feel like it's OK to confess to you that I re-gifted once. Do you know what that is? It's when you give a gift to someone that once was given to you. It was a glass candy dish we received for our wedding. It was beautiful, but my wife and I saw no future for that dish in our lives, so when we were guests at a wedding a couple of years later and a few dozen dollars below the poverty line, we decided to look for a gift a little closer to home. So we went to the closet and selected the nice glass bowl and the box that had never been opened.

I still regret re-gifting. That couple deserved our best. We spent nothing on them. What does that say about us? What does that say about them? I wouldn't re-gift my brother. I wouldn't re-gift my mom. I wouldn't even re-gift my mother-in-law, nor would I suggest it. And I definitely wouldn't re-gift Jesus.

He deserves the best we have, not some afterthought we find way back in some corner of our closet. That's exactly what Mary thought, too. Not *that* Mary. The other Mary.

We all know that Mary, the mother of our Jesus, was forever changed by the manger, but did you know that there was another Mary who was changed by the manger? Matthew doesn't name the woman who gave Jesus an amazing gift at the home of Simon the Leper, but John tells us that her name was Mary, the sister of Martha and Lazarus (John 12:1–8). This Mary wasn't there when Jesus inhaled air for the first time, but she was there when Jesus called her brother's name, "Lazarus," and he began to inhale air for the first time—again. She saw his power, his love, and his tears. She loved him. He saved her brother and he saved her, too.

She wasn't there to give him a gift at his birth, but she wanted to give him a gift before his death robbed her of the opportunity, so she gave him one of the best gifts in the history of gifts. As Jesus reclined at the table, Mary poured very expensive perfume on Christ's head. It was worth about a year's wages, so, by today's standards, she poured about $30,000 worth of perfume on Christ's head.

The disciples, led by Judas, were beside themselves, "Why this waste?" they asked. Judas, who was probably a re-gifter, and the other disciples didn't understand the extravagance of the gift. It appeared to be too much. Surely Jesus, knowing the number of poor people sitting on street corners and beside wells in Jerusalem, would rebuke this senseless waste of money.

Just the opposite. Jesus praised her and promised that "Wherever this gospel is preached throughout the world, what she has done will also be told, in memory of her."

Why did Jesus praise this woman for such an apparent "waste" of expensive perfume and promise that her story would be told until the end of time? Because she did what we all should do. She gave Jesus the best she had. She gave her best because God did the same for her . . . and for us.

When God sent his son to this world as a baby he gave us his very best. God loved us so much that He gave us a priceless gift—his son—wrapped carefully in a manger with a tag that read, "For the World." And for this, and a million other reasons, God deserves our best and not our loose change.

—Arron Chambers

Spiritual Lessons in Action

Give Jesus a great gift. Maybe you need to write a large check to your house of worship. Maybe you need to make a donation of new clothes, supplies, or toys to a family who is in need. Maybe God's been calling you to do something amazing for Him. Maybe God's calling you to do something that your family, or friends, may disagree with. Make this a wondrous day by giving your best gift to Jesus, now.

Mercy at 10,000 Feet

By Paul "Doc" Johnson

Have mercy on me, O God, have mercy on me, for in you my soul takes refuge. I will take refuge in the shadow of your wings until the disaster has passed. I cry out to God Most High, to God, who fulfills [his purpose] for me. He sends from heaven and saves me, rebuking those who hotly pursue me; God sends his love and his faithfulness.

I am in the midst of lions; I lie among ravenous beasts—men whose teeth are spears and arrows, whose tongues are sharp swords. Be exalted, O God, above the heavens; let your glory be over all the earth. They spread a net for my feet—I was bowed down in distress. They dug a pit in my path—but they have fallen into it themselves. My heart is steadfast, O God, my heart is steadfast; I will sing and make music. Awake, my soul! Awake, harp and lyre! I will awaken the dawn. I will praise you, O Lord, among the nations; I will sing of you among the peoples. For great is your love, reaching to the heavens; your faithfulness reaches to the skies. Be exalted, O God, above the heavens; let your glory be over all the earth.

—PSALM 57

I am an old man now, eighty-one years old. But as the Christmas season approaches, I often think of this story. I haven't always been old. Back in 1944, I was a young man, surely full of myself, with not much modesty.

I was a fighter pilot in the Thirty-Fifth Fighter Group, twenty years old, and a captain in the old Army Air Corps (the predecessor to the U.S. Air Force). With four kills already, only one more needed to be a combat ace, false modesty did not become me, though it does not become any fighter pilot. You must always think of yourself as invincible. It's what keeps you alive. I have never talked to a fighter pilot who didn't think he was the best. How could we all be the best? I don't know, but it does seem a mindset that fighter pilots have. I've known many of my peers over the years, and it seems that we all had the same affliction. It carries over into your life in general, too. I know even in my advanced years, not once have I ever heard "Doc, you sure are a modest man." Be that as it may, since I have become a follower of Jesus in the Christian Church, I have tried hard to be a meek and mild fellow. I do the best I can.

So, back to Christmas morning in 1944. We had taken off from our base thirty-five miles southwest of London. We had the job of protecting the B-17 formations that were wreaking havoc on the German heartland. The B-17s would take off about 4:00 A.M. from their respective bases, and we would follow them about two hours behind because our speed would make up the difference. We caught up to the bombers close to the Dutch–German border.

There was not much activity over Holland and France that day, but when we reached the German border, it was much different. There were plenty of enemy fighter planes—all you'd care to see.

I was a Roman Catholic then, and I had taken communion that morning from a good friend, Father Worachak, a Polish priest assigned to our group. He was a most remarkable young man. He would stand on the flight line as about fifty P-51 Ds taxied down the runway, taking off two at a time. When he would spot one of "his boys," he would jump up on the wing, you would slide the canopy back, he would say a prayer and pop a wafer in your mouth, and presto, you had communion. He sure had guts. I really liked him.

The P-51 D was a remarkable tool. It was a great airplane that cruised at about 300 mph. Twenty years old, with all that power in your hands—no wonder we felt invincible. I was flying a million-dollar airplane, and I hadn't learned to drive a car yet.

The P-51s were powered with the Rolls Royce's "Merlin" engine, built by the Packard Motor Car Company in the United States. Ever hear one run? It's the only sound I know that beats the roar of a Harley-Davidson motorcycle.

We were flying in a V formation, a lead plane and two other planes on either side—a total of five planes altogether. Looking out ahead, we saw a very similar formation heading toward us. Major Jacobs gave the signal to break formation, and we began to peel off, one by one. I had picked my target and I began to eyeball him.

I flew combat later in Korea, flying the much faster F-86, but no one ever was so formidable an adversary as a crack German pilot in an FW 190. In a dogfight you do just about that—fight like dogs—circling around, trying to find his soft spot, and then you both back off, and several miles apart you begin your attack. You fly straight at each other for a few seconds and try to align your sights. I had been taught to conserve ammunition, so I usually stood back and waited for my adversary to fire first. If your adversary was firing at you, you would see his wing light up like a blue neon sign. We got closer and closer . . . but still, no telltale blue line.

He wasn't firing and neither was I. I couldn't believe my eyes. Suddenly we began to pass each other. Was I seeing what I thought I was seeing? Was he waving at me as he zipped past?

We were moving so fast I couldn't tell. Then he did an abrupt 180-degree turn, and I realized he was coming slowly up my port side. I slowed to let him catch up. I was fascinated. It was almost dreamlike. He flew alongside for several seconds so close I could see his face. He looked older than I was, maybe in his forties. I saw lots of stars below his canopy, denoting those of us he had shot down. He was obviously a veteran pilot, flying circles around me. He inched closer to me, so close I swear I could see his instrument panel.

As we flew alongside each other I could see he was waving at me. I didn't know what else to do, so I waved back. I could see he was laughing all the while, then he peeled off—and was gone.

I have always felt that God gave me the gift of life that Christmas morning over Germany and, in that instant, I was transformed from a boy to a man. From that point I committed to make my life mean something. I gave my heart to the Lord and have tried all my life to be the kind of man God would be proud of.

I have often wondered whatever happened to that pilot. Did he survive the war, as I did, or was he killed? Did he get to do the things I got to do? Did he get to raise a great family, as I did? Did he get to marry his Peggy, as I did?

I'll never know, but about every time I take communion in Church, among my friends and church family, especially at Christmas time, my heart says a prayer for his immortal soul. God gave me a chance, on a cold morning in 1944—Christmas morning—in the sky over Germany . . . a chance at a better life. I hope I have succeeded. I sure hope so. God bless us, every one.

✝ *The Pastor Says* . . .

Have you ever felt like you were going to die and there was nothing you could do about it?

My brother found out on a Wednesday that he had a brain tumor. Five days later, we were in his apartment praying that somehow, some way, God would answer our prayers and save his life.

His surgery was set for early the next morning. The surgeon, one of only six in the country able to perform that particular surgery, told us that Adam's chances were not good. He had percentages to help us understand that my brother was going to either die or be drastically changed, but he was not going to be the same. So, we gathered in my brother's apartment, to pray to God and sing the fear out. My brother spent the majority of that night praying in a closet. He prayed for healing, strength, and mercy from certain death.

David wasn't in a closet—it was a cave, and he too, was facing certain death. King Saul was jealous of the attention that David received after killing Goliath. He allowed this jealousy to work like venom and poison his soul. One morning, under the influence of an evil spirit, Saul tried to kill David with a spear. David was playing a harp one minute, and running for his life the next. David fled and hid in a cave.

Saul was the most powerful person in the world, so David knew that to leave the cave would be certain death. As he faced death, from the depths of a cave he cried out, "Have mercy on me, O God, have mercy on me" (Ps. 57:1).

He needed mercy—and God delivered him from the hands of his enemy. David was delivered to lead a nation and a legacy.

I was facing certain death, too. Not from a tumor, a king, or a German ace. I was facing certain death at the hands of my sin. I thought I was doomed, until mercy showed up in the person of Jesus.

I went into ministry.

Paul Johnson flew home.

And Adam got married last June.

My brother survived and spent several years learning how to walk, talk, and live again, but now Adam has two master's degrees and will be earning a Ph.D., in the next year. He's a professor, and the husband to the girl of his dreams—who just happens to be a doctor. God is good, isn't He?

—Arron Chambers

Spiritual Lessons in Action

Start listing how God has been good to you. Now, read your list as a prayer to God, saying, "Lord, thank you for . . ." before each item.

Stunning Coincidence

By Twila Sias

Some time later God tested Abraham. He said to him, "Abraham!" "Here I am," he replied. Then God said, "Take your son, your only son, Isaac, whom you love, and go to the region of Moriah. Sacrifice him there as a burnt offering on one of the mountains I will tell you about."

Early the next morning Abraham got up and saddled his donkey. He took with him two of his servants and his son Isaac. When he had cut enough wood for the burnt offering, he set out for the place God had told him about. On the third day Abraham looked up and saw the place in the distance. He said to his servants, "Stay here with the donkey while I and the boy go over there. We will worship and then we will come back to you." Abraham took the wood for the burnt offering and placed it on his son Isaac, and he himself carried the fire and the knife.

As the two of them went on together, Isaac spoke up and said to his father Abraham, "Father?"

"Yes, my son?" Abraham replied.

"The fire and wood are here," Isaac said, "but where is the lamb for the burnt offering?"

Abraham answered, "God himself will provide the lamb for the burnt offering, my son." And the two of them went on together. When they reached the place God had told him about, Abraham built an altar there and arranged the wood on it. He bound his son Isaac and laid him on the altar, on top of the wood. Then he reached out his hand and took the knife to slay his son. But the angel of the LORD called out to him from heaven, "Abraham! Abraham!"

"Here I am," he replied. "Do not lay a hand on the boy," he said. "Do not do anything to him. Now I know that you fear God, because you have not withheld from me your son, your only son." Abraham looked up and there in a thicket he saw a ram caught by its horns. He went over and took the ram and sacrificed it as a burnt offering instead of his son. So Abraham called that place The LORD Will Provide. And to this day it is said, "On the mountain of the LORD it will be provided."

—GENESIS 22:1–14

It's not easy, living with people of faith. Life is often wonderful, but seldom easy.

I grew up in a rural community of southern Illinois with two parents, three brothers, and an assortment of pets. We lived off a country road in a parsonage, separated from a church building— white, wood frame, with a steeple—by a gravel parking lot.

We experienced the poverty that is typical for many preachers' families. Even as the oldest child, I maintained a wardrobe of hand-me-down clothing, most of which I would never have chosen. We planted a garden in the side yard, canned our vegetables, and drank powdered milk. Neighbors and relatives occasionally butchered a cow or hog and would share a portion of meat. Dad bought an electric hair clipper and created his own hair-cutting corner in our basement, where he did cuts for himself, my three brothers, and sometimes neighbors or guys from church who would drop by "just to chat." For most of these men, the major part of social life centered around church or the grain elevator, so sitting on a stool in someone's basement, enjoying friendly conversation, had some appeal.

As is true for many children, my brothers and I didn't know we were poor. While our friends received new bicycles for birthdays, we rode really cool stuff that Dad had welded together from an assortment of parts, scavenged from the local junkyard. After some creative paint jobs and a couple of fancy attachments purchased new from the hardware store, we were proud owners of bikes and playground equipment no one else had. Ironically, some children envied our stuff and our life.

Even with an income at poverty level, we didn't display some of the usual signs of the underprivileged. We went to school in clean, ironed clothing. Even when the well was dry, with water for only one bath per week, Mom made sure we were sponged clean every day so we were presentable for school. During summer months, we washed up in a creek or swam in a gravel pit. Somehow our parents made every lacking turn into a gift—or an occasion for fun.

Through my teenage years, I grew more aware of our financial challenges—and a bit more envious of my friends' homes and possessions. I also developed a growing frustration with my parents and the life of sacrifice they had chosen. My parents had great respect for people who had the gift and the drive to earn large amounts of money—and a special appreciation for those whose generous hearts were tuned in to the needs of others. It's just that they had chosen a life where hard work was not typically rewarded with substantial salaries.

Throughout our senior year of high school, my friends and I eagerly planned for college. Most friends had parents who—over a number of years—had been socking away thousands of dollars for their kids' college educations. Well . . . I knew that hadn't been happening in my case.

I kept bugging Mom for reassurance that college was truly in my future, and she kept saying, "God has always provided every need." She never had much else to say on the subject. That was that. No explanations necessary. God's track record was obviously supposed to speak for itself.

To add to the financial intrigue, that year our church had decided to put its collective and individual faith to the test. Individuals and families put their faith to the test—their faith in God's ability to provide—by promising to give a designated amount of money over the following year to missions and the needs of others, both in the United States and around the world. To many, these "steps of faith" surely seemed foolish, but my parents were accustomed to seeing evidence of God's provision for everyday needs throughout their life together.

The day came to turn in the pledge cards. My parents—together—had agreed on an amount of $1,000 from our family, but the one thing they had not discussed was who would fill out the card. Unfortunately, they both filled out a card, inadvertently doubling our family commitment. During a rather lively dinner conversation that evening, this oversight came clear.

"I thought I was filling out the pledge card."

"No . . . remember? I said I would do it."

"Well, it's not really a problem," and Dad went on to offer his solution. "I'll just let the pledge committee know that we made a mistake, and they'll reduce the amount from the total."

This all seemed reasonable to me. After all, how could our family come up with money to fulfill a double pledge? I didn't see how we'd come up with an extra one thousand dollars over the next year, let alone two thousand.

But people are full of surprises. Mom's chuckle turned into outright, uninhibited laughter. "Are you kidding? A thousand dollars is totally impossible. If God can provide one thousand dollars for us to give, He can just as easily provide two!"

"Hmm . . . that's true." "No mistake—one thousand or two— it's all God's provision. Well . . . Why not?"

Oh, no. I groaned inwardly but kept my opinion to myself. This plan had "disaster" plastered all over it, but the folks seemed completely energized by the possibilities, eager to see how God would honor their promises.

And throughout that year, He did honor their promises. Somehow the money for the additional offering was always available—just enough, just in time. That year, we worked three gardens, so we spent almost nothing at the grocery. We all had unexpected opportunities for small odd jobs. Neighbors increasingly dropped off meat, milk, or bread. The shoes didn't seem to wear out as quickly. Every day, there seemed to be some incredible coincidence that gave us what we needed. We couldn't really explain how it happened. We just knew that at the end of the commitment period, our family had fulfilled the double promise.

Actually, God had provided. I should have learned from a lifetime of these experiences, but after all, they weren't my promises, and the lessons from incredible coincidences were secondhand. Besides, I still yearned for college and was consumed with my own plans.

That August, I headed to college, proud that my first semester was paid for with a combination of funding from state scholarships and my entire savings. I hadn't looked past the first semester. If I could just get there, somehow the momentum of college would just carry me along. I had no idea how to finish the second semester, let alone three more years.

When it was preregistration day for spring term, my bill came up $200 short. OK—so you're thinking $200: no big deal. At that time, $200 might as well have been $2,000.

Christmas break came. I stewed over the problem. The folks didn't seem worried. "What good is it to worry?" Mom's opinion didn't help. "There isn't anything we can do that we're not already doing, and worry isn't going to solve the problem."

The weekend before the new semester rolled around quickly. Panic set in, but the folks remained calm. Sunday arrived, in other words, the day before Monday, the start of the new term . . . the absolute due date for my school bill. I had already started planning my appeal to the college business office—a plea for an extension to be paid off from my part-time work.

That's when the call came. It had nothing to do with me. A neighbor wanted Dad's help with an unusual situation. The caller didn't explain, just made an appointment to come to our house that evening.

His family situation had been tragic. The year before, he and his family had been in a horrible car accident while on vacation; a driver had been asleep at the wheel. Several of his family had suffered severe injuries. One child had died.

The insurance settlement arrived but certainly brought no consolation. In fact, the neighbor and his wife had decided to give the money away. They knew Dad and Mom had contact with missionaries all around the world: people who built medical clinics, schools, orphanages, churches; people committed to enriching the lives of others physically, mentally, and spiritually. These neighbors wanted names and addresses of worthy recipients who would use the funds wisely, to the best purposes.

The couple sat at our kitchen table writing checks—totaling thousands of dollars—to be distributed to people in need around the globe. They collected mailing addresses and, after a couple of hours, headed home to write letters to accompany their gifts.

As they stood on the porch exchanging a last little dribble of conversation, the neighbor turned to Dad, handed him a folded check, and said, "You know, I really appreciate your good heart and everything you do for others. Please don't argue. Here's a little something for you from a grateful friend."

These generous neighbors drove away, and Dad came back into the house. "Well, they are delightful people!" Mom had enjoyed the evening and could already anticipate the excitement and surprise of at least a dozen people around the world who would soon receive an unexpected blessing.

"Yeah, what a thrill to be around people with such huge hearts. Oh, I almost forgot." He dug the folded check out of his shirt pocket. "He gave me this."

"What is it?" my mother asked.

"I didn't look. Here, you take it"—and Dad walked off to the kitchen with not so much as a lick of curiosity.

Mom opened the folded check, smiled, and handed it to me. "Here, honey. I think this is yours."

Two hundred dollars—no more, no less. Just the right amount. Just the right time. Stunning . . . absolutely stunning.

✝ *The Pastor Says* . . .

I know if I could have seen with God's eyes, I would have found certain words written on his heart.

My grandfather and grandmother spent their lives tearing down walls and destroying strongholds. No, they weren't in the destruction business; they were in the ministry. Specifically, they helped African Americans to build churches from the 1950s through the 1980s. They would help in the raising of money, purchasing of church buildings, and training of staff. Their ministry was challenging, but rewarding. They knew no fear and had no doubts that God's hand of blessing was on them.

My grandfather could speak for days telling stories of what God had done for them. Let me tell you one.

Grandma had been in the hospital with tuberculosis. She had a lung removed and endured a lengthy hospital stay. Grandma had befriended many of the women on the mostly

African American nursing staff at the hospital in Denver, Colorado. She respected them, and they returned the favor.

The day came for Grandma to check out and for the bill to be paid. The financial director, who was also African American, called my grandfather into her office, pulled the shades, and began to speak softly. "Mr. Maxey, the bill for your wife's hospital stay comes to about $35,000 (this was 1981). Now, we've decided that since we tested so many new medications and procedures on your wife, her expenses should be written off. We'll have to charge you for some incidentals. We figure you owe us about $300. How would you like to pay your bill?"

Grandpa, afraid she'd change her mind, or he'd wake up, quickly replied, "I'll write a check."

Abraham can relate. He saw the Lord step in at the perfect time and provide. God told him to take his son to a mountain in the region of Moriah and sacrifice him there. In faith, Abraham took Isaac to the place of sacrificing, assuring him that "God himself will provide the lamb for the burnt offering" (Gen. 22:8). And God did, at just the right moment. As the knife was preparing to slice flesh, Abraham looked up and saw a ram caught in a nearby thicket.

I've had the same experience. My wife and I were preparing to have our third child and realized that our four-door, highly unreliable car was a problem. We prayed that God would help us find a reliable car at an affordable price.

Within weeks, someone showed up at our house at 9:00 P.M. on a Saturday night with a minivan for us. Not to borrow, but to have—they were giving it to us. Praise God!

That's only one of the many reasons why it is written across my heart. And it's the same thing that's written across

Abraham's heart, Grandpa's heart, and Twila's heart, too. "The Lord will provide."

—Arron Chambers

Spiritual Lessons in Action

Get a pad of sticky notes. Write "The Lord will provide" on one and put it on the inside flap of your checkbook. Write "The Lord will provide" on another one, and place it on the outside of your refrigerator. Write "The Lord will provide" on another one and place it on the dashboard of your car. Get the idea? Write "The Lord will provide" and place this truth anywhere and everywhere you need to be reminded of this truth.

Bluff Cave and the Devil Dogs

By Andrew Peterson

They came back to Moses and Aaron and the whole Israelite community at Kadesh in the Desert of Paran. There they reported to them and to the whole assembly and showed them the fruit of the land. They gave Moses this account: "We went into the land to which you sent us, and it does flow with milk and honey! Here is its fruit. But the people who live there are powerful, and the cities are fortified and very large. We even saw descendants of Anak there. The Amalekites live in the Negev; the Hittites, Jebusites and Amorites live in the hill country; and the Canaanites live near the sea and along the Jordan."

Then Caleb silenced the people before Moses and said, "We should go up and take possession of the land, for we can certainly do it."

—NUMBERS 13:26—30

Our first mistake was trying to find the cave in the middle of the night. That, to a normal person, would've been obvious, but alas, we were five college students who had not yet grown in the wisdom and stature of the Lord.

It was the hottest part of the summer in East Tennessee. A youth conference had descended on the local Christian college, so church vans from all over the Southeast with white-stenciled church names on the sides were lined up in rows in the college parking lot. I can't remember why I was there. I'm pretty sure I was helping out at the conference in some capacity. I was also partly there to visit friends, and that's where the trouble set in.

My friend Mack, a youth minister with an uncanny knack for making quick friends with the locals, found out about a hidden cave somewhere nearby called Bluff Cave. Rumor had it that the cave was a mile deep, easy to navigate, and if you went far enough into it, there was an underground lake, complete with blind catfish the length of your arm. All you had to do was drive deep into the hills of Tennessee to a secluded trailer park, sneak across some private property into the woods, and follow the arrows painted on the tree trunks. It was as easy as that. Frankly, with a setup like that for an adventure, I had no choice. I was going to spelunk, by golly, and that was that.

All we had to do was wait until we had some free time at the youth conference, make sure the kids in our charge were well chaperoned, then slip away to the infamous cave. Mack and I scouted the area that afternoon. After several wrong turns and a thirty-minute drive down those winding Tennessee back roads, we found the trailer park.

The trailer park didn't feel threatening during the day. The sun was bright, the birds were singing, and we didn't feel like we were in too much danger. If the locals were suspicious of a strange van in their neighborhood, they had but to notice the church moniker on the side and they could return to whatever they were doing. So Mack and I parked the van where he'd been instructed to by his contact.

We set out across a wide yard where the ugliest dog in America was chained to a large hickory tree. It was one of those chow dogs that hadn't been brushed in years; its matted fur hung down in tick-laden locks of reddish brown hair. Its purple tongue lolled out the side of its mouth, and the hairs on my neck stood on end at the thought of that beast licking its chops with that very tongue after feasting on my innards. Well, the dog smelled my fear, I reckon, because it leapt to its feet and lunged in our direction, snapping the chain taut. If this were a tall tale, I'd tell you that the tree actually bent and five squirrels fell out.

The dog set to howling and snarling at us, and we worried that the person whose yard we were cutting through might come out to investigate. After thirty long seconds, we made it to the woods and relaxed. Not long after, we found the arrows painted on the trees, just as Mack's contact had described. The woods were thick, and there were traces of a path that led to the next arrow, and so on. Even so, we lost our way several times and had to backtrack to find the arrow we'd missed.

Finally, in a deep gully, hidden by brush and thickets, we saw the gaping mouth of the cave. We cheered and scrambled down to the fifty-foot opening, and my heart pounded with excitement. I looked at my watch, and my heart thudded with disappointment. Time had flown, and we had to leave to get back in time for our responsibilities at the youth conference. Mack and I looked at each other, then at the cave, then back at each other. We knew what had to be done. "We're coming back," I said.

"Tonight," he said.

And we were off at a trot, back through the woods, back past the beast with the purple tongue, back to the church van, and back to the youth conference. In between seminars and worship services, we recruited three more friends to join us in our spelunking foolishness.

The five of us—two women, three men—planned to meet at the specified church van at the specified time, well after everyone else was asleep. That way we could explore the cave to our hearts' content, the only casualty being our alertness the next day. I figured it wouldn't make any difference if we were in the cave in the middle of the night or at noon, since it would be pitch black in there anyway. All we needed was to make a trip to the local twenty-four-hour Wal-Mart to get some rope, a few flashlights, and some garbage bags in which to put our muddy clothes after the spelunk.

At about 2:00 A.M., we turned into the trailer park, and as we eased through, a family of skunks crossed the road. The van squeaked to a stop, and we all peeked through the front windshield at them while the momma skunk and four baby skunks toddled across the road, unperturbed by the headlights trained on them. The girls thought they were cute. I thought they were an omen.

The skunk clan disappeared into the brush, and we continued, looking nervously at the many, many old pickups parked in front of the trailers. Every truck was rusted, decorated with a Rebel flag, and adorned with a gun rack. I'm sure we all thought about how silly it was that we were in that particular trailer park at 2:00 A.M., far, far from anyone who knew us, but no one said a word; we'd spent good money on those two-dollar flashlights, and to a college student, that meant we were heavily invested in the enterprise. We parked the van at the appointed place and got out, whispering to each other to "close the door quietly" and to "hand me my bag of clothes" and to "lemme have the bug spray." I remember I could hear the sound of a television playing in one of the trailers a few yards away. So far, we hadn't wakened any dogs or their owners. We had yet to make it past the Beast, however.

We had tiptoed halfway across the yard when Purple-Tongued Demon Dog awoke with a fury. It barked madly. We all jumped five feet in the air, and Mack said, "Run!" Behind us, Purple Tongue's army of fellow demon dogs woke, and their barks filled the air as every light in every trailer turned on, and the people of Tennessee ran for their weapons.

Fifteen minutes later, somewhere in Canada, we stopped to catch our breath. We had run blindly through the woods, certain that we were being chased by a legion of horrors, and when we finally stopped, we had no idea where we were. I remember laughing, doubled over, thanking God that I was still alive and intact. We could hear the barks far in the distance, but we weren't being chased. Our relief at being alive turned quickly to ill-placed confidence, and we set out to find the cave. After hours— literally hours— of wandering through the woods, shining our flashlights on trees, and looking for those elusive arrows, we managed to find the cave entrance.

The spelunking was marvelous. I figured that by morning I'd either be eaten by a canine or shot in the gut for trespassing, so the cave exploration was especially sublime. We slipped in the mud, crawled through narrow openings, admired stalagmites, and sat high on a boulder and shone our lights down on the underground lake. Since this isn't a tall tale, I'll tell you that it was more like a pond, but we weren't complaining. We sat in the cave and sang hymns to the God who had made everything on the earth, and our voices echoed off the walls and serenaded the blind fish. It may as well have been the Sistine Chapel. I wish that were the end of the story.

We made our way out of the cave and back to the edge of the woods where our friend, Evil Chow, was waiting. Across the way I could see the dim shape of our trusty steed, the church van, in which we would make our getaway. The dogs were quiet, the trailer lights were off, and unless the tenants of the trailer park had organized a posse and were lying in ambush, we were home free.

We snuck past Cujo's lair, and our spirits lightened. We imagined ourselves crawling into our beds with a great story to tell. But as we approached the van, my heart shriveled in my chest. In the road, between us and our only hope for escape, were about fifteen very angry, very territorial dogs. Their eyes glinted in the moonlight, and when they saw us they all stood and raised their hackles while they growled. None of them had yet barked, presumably because they wanted to eat us without their owners spoiling the fun by shooting us outright. They just stood and growled and edged toward us. It goes without saying that we prayed without ceasing.

That's when it occurred to me just how suspicious we must have looked. Five of us were in the middle of the road, covered with mud from head to toe. We were all carrying sticks (which could've been easily mistaken for rifles), and garbage bags (which could've easily been mistaken for bags of loot). I imagine that we looked remarkably like the burglars in *101 Dalmatians*, covered in soot.

"The skunks!" I said. "We should've known when we saw the skunks!"

The others looked at me blankly. I'm not saying I was making any sense at this point. Several plans were presented and dismissed, and the five of us were seriously considering going back to live out our lives in Bluff Cave. I was sure we could subsist quite happily on blind catfish. Mack was an ordained minister, so we could marry off and populate the cave until we had raised up an army capable of defeating the Beast and his horde. It would take years, but it could work. It had to work.

Or, we could do the unthinkable and ask for help. At about 4:00 A.M., Mack and I very timidly knocked on the door of the least hostile-looking trailer we could find. We stood about ten feet back from the door with our hands up, assuming that the tenant would be armed and groggy. A sleepy-looking gentleman opened the door and eyed us for a long moment.

"Gone cavin' have ya?" he said.

We stuttered an affirmation. "Yes—yessir," I said. "And there are all these dogs, see, and we can't get to our van, and—"

"Dogs?" he asked, looking down the hill behind us where the others were holding a passionate prayer meeting on our account. He rolled his eyes. "Those pups won't hurt you boys. I'll turn on the porch light here, and you all just walk on to yer van." And he was gone.

If this was a tall tale, I'd tell you that we had to wrestle the gun from the crazy old man, and that I used it to blaze a trail through the pack of wild dogs. I'd tell you that I held the beasts at bay screaming, "Women first!" while my comrades scrambled into the van, and that we peeled away, nearly running over a mother skunk holding a picket sign that said "The end is near."

But this is a true story. All we had to do was trust what the kind old man on the hill told us. Our senses, oddly enough, were misinformed by our imaginations, and in truth we had nothing at all to fear as we walked through the puppies—yes, puppies—to our van.

✝ The Pastor Says . . .

Some people don't see what other people see. Some look at the glass and they see enough water, but others don't see enough.

My wife's uncle Fred is one of those who always sees the glass as having more than enough water, even if only a drop remains. It's not that he has that much faith in the drop; it's that he has that much faith in God.

Fred, who ministers in Jacksonville, Florida, was a preacher. He faithfully served the same church for over forty years. During that time they started ten churches. Where others saw a challenge, Uncle Fred saw an opportunity. It takes a lot of work—and faith—to start one church, let alone ten.

Almost thirty years ago, Uncle Fred had a vision for a bible college in central Florida. He began praying and working to see this dream become a reality. He was told again and again that there was no way he was going to be able to start a bible college, but Uncle Fred doesn't see what others see.

One day a woman gave Fred a check for $3,000 to start that bible college he'd been talking about. He took that money and put it to work for God. And in 1975, Central Florida Bible College (now Florida Christian College) began meeting in a church building. Now, thirty years later, Florida Christian College sits on a beautiful forty-acre multimillion-dollar campus in Kissimmee, Florida, and is a fully accredited Christian college training men and women for ministry from the church to the school to the mission field to the workplace. Fred saw a college where others saw only a cow pasture and mosquitoes.

Fred reminds me of Caleb. Caleb and eleven other men were sent by Moses to explore the land of Canaan. The Israelites had been wandering for forty years and were just about to enter the land God promised to them back when their parents were slaves in Egypt. When the twelve spies came back from exploring the land, they reported that the land was wonderful.

"It does flow with milk and honey," they reported (Num. 13:27). But they continued, "The people who live there are powerful, and the cities are fortified and very large. We even saw the descendants of Anak there" (Num. 13:28).

Caleb's faith was bigger than any giants living in any land. He silenced the people and said, "We should go up and take possession of the land, for we can certainly do it" (Num. 13:30).

They did do it and we can, too. We are surrounded by giants: giant diseases, giant financial problems, giant family issues, giant wars, giant storms, and giant fears, but we must see those "giants" for what they really are. These giants are tiny when compared with the bigness of God.

When you look at the "giants" in your land, remember that God has already promised the land to all of his children, so even though we face fear we must have faith that we can certainly do it. Every day, we must see victory when others see defeat. We must see opportunity when others see an obstacle. We must see the Promised Land when others see giants. And we must see puppies when others see devil dogs.

—Arron Chambers

Spiritual Lessons in Action

List the top five challenges you are facing right now, and after each challenge write, "We can certainly do it!"

The Day God Walked Me Home from School

By Molly Noble Bull

Humble yourselves, therefore, under God's mighty hand, that he may lift you up in due time. Cast all your anxiety on him because he cares for you.

Be self-controlled and alert. Your enemy the devil prowls around like a roaring lion looking for someone to devour. Resist him, standing firm in the faith, because you know that your brothers throughout the world are undergoing the same kind of sufferings.

—I PETER 5:6—9

As we travel down the road of life, we all experience events that affect the rest of our lives. Mine took place the moment I stepped onto the curb in front of my elementary school in Corpus Christi, Texas. I was waiting for the light to change. I don't remember the day, the month, the year, or whether I was in the second or third grade.

Back then, little girls wore dresses to school and durable leather shoes, and my mother had made me a dress in a different color for every day of the week. My brown hair was long and wavy, and I wore hair bows and socks that matched my dresses. I carried a handheld book satchel in pink and blue plaid where I kept my tablet, my pencil, and any papers I had done that day.

I remember seeing a gray sedan parked across the street, and I'd never seen a car parked there before. A sense of danger swept through me, and I thought of going home another way. But when the light changed, I crossed South Alameda like I always did.

It's amazing what details a person can recall at times like this. I have no idea what had gone on at school that day, but I remember that the sidewalk was about three feet from the street. Green grass, recently mowed, connected the sidewalk to the curb. The man had parked his car as close to the curb as he could get it, and I saw him looking at me in his rearview mirror as soon as I stepped onto the sidewalk.

He had black hair, and looking at the back of his head, I noticed that his cheeks were puffed out at the sides like he was grinning, or maybe laughing at me. As I moved closer, I saw a tan blazer draped over the back of the seat on the passenger side, and the window closest to me had been rolled down.

"Would you like a ride, little girl?"

My heart pulled into a hard knot. He had a pleasant-sounding voice. But somehow, I knew I needed to run.

"No!" I started running.

My mother had told me never to ride with strangers or even talk to them. As I raced down the sidewalk in the direction of our garage apartment, I tried to understand what was happening.

Mama never told me what to do after I refused the offer of a ride. I had assumed the stranger would say something like "You don't want a ride? Well, okay. Good-bye." Then he would drive off.

But he wheeled as close to that curb as he could and braked his gray sedan to a crawl, keeping pace with me as I sprinted down the sidewalk. My heart pounded, and I didn't stop at the first intersection. Terrified, I ran across the street without looking for oncoming cars, but as I approached the second intersection, I considered turning right after I crossed the street instead of continuing down the sidewalk. I could walk between houses until I reached an alley I knew about, and then run down the alley until I got home.

A voice in my head said, "No, Molly. Just keep running down the sidewalk."

I did exactly as the voice said and kept going. However, I soon realized that I needed to slow down or I would dash right by our apartment. I reduced my speed and hurried across the three driveways in front of our house. When the man saw that I was walking fast instead of running, he stopped his car about forty feet ahead of me next to the tall grass.

There was a vacant lot next to our garage apartment, and the grass on the lot and the grass between the sidewalk and the street hadn't been cut in a long time. My head and shoulders barely showed above the weeds when I walked down that sidewalk.

A stairway to the side of the garage apartment had a landing about three or four steps up. I climbed the stairs two at a time without looking back. At the landing, the stairs went up the back of the building to a porch where the doors were located. I grabbed the handle on the screen door and pulled as hard as I could, but the door wouldn't open. How could I have forgotten that my mother always kept it locked?

"Mama," I shouted. "Let me in! A man is after me."

In the time it took for her to open the door, I looked down. The man stood on the landing, peering up at me. I felt trapped, and fear devoured me.

He wore a short-sleeved white shirt and dark trousers, and he had dark eyes and a black mustache. I couldn't define that look he sent me then. Now, I know it was pure lust.

My mother opened the door, and I raced inside.

Mama went out on the porch, perhaps to find out what was going on. The man said, "I just wanted to tell you, lady, what a cute little girl you have."

"Thank you," she said. "We think so, too."

Then the man turned, got in his car, and roared off.

At the time, Mama didn't know what happened earlier. Therefore, she didn't even try to get his license plate number. However, she walked me to and from school after that.

I've heard it said that events like this hardly bother children at all. Not true. I had disturbing dreams for years and years, and the effects of this encounter didn't end there. My best friend in high school liked guys who were tall, dark, and handsome. But boys I admired had to have either blue or green eyes, and brown or blond hair, like my dad. My favorite movie actors were Paul Newman and later Mel Gibson instead of a dark Cary Grant type, and I thought this was a personal choice, like liking chocolate ice cream and hating red beets. I just wasn't attracted to boys with dark eyes and black hair, and if a young man with a mustache looked in my direction, forget it.

What happened that day changed my life—forever. Yet I can't stop wondering what my life would have been like if the man with the black mustache had been successful. I am married, and we have three grown sons and four grandchildren. Would I ever have married if things had turned out differently? Would I be writing this true story? Or would I be in a mental institution? Or perhaps in a cemetery somewhere in Corpus Christi, Texas?

I cannot say why some children are captured by evil men, while others are not. I only know that God spoke to me that day so long ago and told me what to do as He walked me home from school. He protected me from all harm, and I praise Him for it. I am glad I obeyed my mother that day and didn't ride with a stranger, and I am thankful that I listened to what I believe was the voice of the Lord.

✝ *The Pastor Says* . . .

We sometimes make jokes out of things that scare us. I think it's how we cope.

I have a lot of pleasant memories from Sunday school. I remember how exciting flannel graph lessons were. Flannel graphs are pictures of Bible characters backed with coarse cloth or similar material that, when pressed on to a sloping board covered with rough material, will not slide off.

Mrs. Tobin could make each flannel graph character sound so realistic. I still hear Mrs. Tobin's voice when I read the words of Mary in the Gospels.

I loved the lessons. I loved using paste, Popsicle sticks, and cotton balls to make sheep. I loved the songs. We sang all of the classics: "Make Me a Sunbeam," "I'm in the Lord's Army," "Jesus Loves Me," "This Little Light of Mine," and "Oh, You Can't Get to Heaven" (which, now that I think about it, has a discouraging title).

Several of these songs talk about the Devil, and in the lyrics pronounce that the Devil should "sit on a tack," be shot with a "gospel gun," and not be allowed to blow out our "little light." The older I've become, the more I've wanted to have the Devil do a lot more than sit on a tack. I despise what he does to families, children, lives, careers, churches, and dreams. As a minister, I've had to walk in after the Devil walked out, and then help people sift hope out of the rubble he left behind.

The Apostle Peter tried to warn us, "Your enemy the devil prowls around like a roaring lion looking for someone to devour" (I Peter 5:8). The Christians to whom Peter was writing were being persecuted, so they understood what lions could do to people. (The emperor Nero, who was ruling Rome at this time, routinely fed Christians to lions.)

Unlike in the Colosseum, in the wild, lions only roar once they have captured their prey. How many gazelles could a lion eat if he walked around roaring all of the time? Only the ones who weren't being careful.

The Devil hates us and wakes up every day committed to devouring us. He's hungry for us, and he wants to catch us in a moment of weakness.

I want you to make today a wondrous day, but the Devil wants this day to be a disaster. You must be alert. He doesn't always drive a gray sedan, as he did in this last story. Sometimes he approaches disguised as an opportunity. Sometimes he comes in a bottle. Sometimes he looks like a credit card. Sometimes he looks like a blonde in a miniskirt. Sometimes he asks you out to lunch when your husband is out of town. He may approach you disguised as a pop-up ad on a Web site. He may try to meet you at a bar, or a movie theater, or even in the back pew at church, so we must always be on our guard.

Like a pedophile searching for an easy victim, Satan is stalking us, so follow Peter's advice—and Molly's example—and "be self-controlled and alert" (I Peter 5:8), remembering that he sometimes looks like a dark-eyed man driving a gray sedan—and his roar sometimes sounds like a pleasant voice.

—Arron Chambers

Spiritual Lessons in Action

List the three areas of your life in which you sense the possibility of evil. Pray that God will make you alert to such evil, so that you can walk safely home today and every day.

Lost in the Racks

By Dr. Kimberly Boyd

N
ow the tax collectors and "sinners"
were all gathering around to hear
him. But the Pharisees and the teachers of the law muttered, "This man welcomes
sinners and eats with them." Then Jesus told
them this parable: "Suppose one of you has a
hundred sheep and loses one of them. Does he
not leave the ninety-nine in the open country and go after the lost sheep until he finds
it? And when he finds it, he joyfully puts it on
his shoulders and goes home. Then he calls
his friends and neighbors together and says,
'Rejoice with me; I have found my lost sheep.'
I tell you that in the same way there will be
more rejoicing in heaven over one sinner who
repents than over ninety-nine righteous per-
sons who do not need to repent.

—LUKE 15:1—7

"Will the mother of a six-year-old named Kim
please come to the service desk?" If my mother

heard that announcement once, she heard it a hundred times! I'm sure my mother knew the moment she walked out of the house with me, as we headed to the store, that I would get lost. I'm sure every time as we headed out the door a cloud of dread hung over her, but we'd go anyway.

Almost every Saturday, when I was very young, my mother would go shopping and bravely take my sister and me along.

We'd almost always start at the clothing department, which would prove to be a mistake, because this would be the most common place I'd get lost. As my mother shopped, mostly looking and hardly ever buying, my older sister and I would crawl into the middle of the clothing racks. Scurrying from one rack to the next, we would make up all sorts of adventures surrounded by pants, shirts, dresses, and the smell of fabric.

My sister, somehow, had a sense of when my mother was moving on and would join her; however, I did not share that same sense. I wanted to stay in my playhouse and pretend to wear the satiny, shiny, sparkling clothes and entertain my pretend guests. I wanted to stay in my make-believe cave and hide from outside intruders as I watched their shadows go by. I wanted to stay in my car and drive to Niagara Falls or the Grand Canyon. Then it would dawn on me . . . I'd better go catch up with my mother and sister before I get lost, but where were they?

I would look around where I had last seen her . . . around the pants . . . around the shirts. I would look around the dresses—several times each. I would be real quiet to see if I could hear my sister. Then I'd start running from aisle to aisle to find them.

Too late. They're gone. They've left the store without me. I'd search and search, to no avail. And then the tears would start, and, boy, would they start.

How could they leave the store without me? What were they thinking? Would God really let them leave without me? Why didn't they come looking for me? Didn't they miss me? What would Daddy say? Would he make them come back and get me? Certainly my brother would miss me—well, maybe not.

About this time, with tears streaming and a panicked face, I would be spotted by a store clerk, whom I'm sure remembered me from the week before. In between great sobs, I would try to identify myself and explain that my mother had left me, as the very kind and usually elderly looking lady gave me some tissue and tried to console me. After several minutes of blubbering and sputtering, and gasps of breath and lots of tears, I would be assured that my mother had not left the store without me and that we would be reunited.

My mother happened to work at one of the department stores that we would frequent, and it was also the one in which I would most frequently get lost. One of the more memorable times I wandered off from my mother happened on a Friday evening. In fact my father and sister were there, too. My parents were talking with the store manager, who happened to be our next door neighbor. My sister and I were looking through the records, trying to find the latest Osmond Brothers album. After locating it and discovering several other records we wanted, we made our way to the furniture department. We tried out all the chairs and sofas. I liked the vinyl ones best—they were good for sliding across. Having checked on the whereabouts of my parents, who were still in the same place talking with Mr. Johnson, our neighbor and the store manager, I decided that it would be OK if I made my way over to the clothing department—just for a minute, to crawl under the racks. So away I went. I did the usual things: crawling under and between the lines of clothes, exploring from one rack to another, being sure to touch every hanging garment. When I concluded this particular outing,

I had wound up in the men's department. I managed to find my way back to where I left my parents, but they were not there. *Where had they gone? Where was my sister? Did they leave the store without me? When would they realize I wasn't in the car with them?*

After several minutes of searching frantically, I began crying uncontrollably and wandering aimlessly, and this time wandered right into the security guard! He put his hand on my shoulder and bent over and asked, "Are you lost? What is your name?" Through sobs and near hyperventilation, I managed to tell him.

"Oh," he said, "Your mother must be Jo who works in the credit department."

"Yes, yes, that's her. But she's not here anymore. She went home with my father and sister without me!" I explained that I had searched the entire store and that my family was nowhere to be found. He picked me up and carried me to the front of the store to the service desk, with futile attempts to relieve my fears that my family had gone home without me. When we got to the service desk he sat me down on the counter, and a very nice lady handed me a bag of popcorn, which of course worked its magic, and I began to calm. Momentarily, I could hear the now almost-ritual announcement being made, "Would the mother of a six-year-old named Kim please come to the service desk?"

A door behind us opened and I watched in disbelief as my parents and sister walked out of Mr. Johnson's office—where they had been the whole time. I had never thought to look there.

Many, many times, I would hear the announcement being made: "Would the mother of a six-year-old named Kim please come to the service desk?" And sure enough, when she was called my mother would soon appear and claim the six-year-old named Kim. What a comfort for me to realize that she had been there the whole time. She'd never left the store! As we exited the store she would hold my hand tightly, making sure that I was safely in the car for the return ride home. And then the next Saturday would come around. . . .

✝ *The Pastor Says . . .*

A little boy was found walking the aisles of a department store. He seemed to be having a grand time. A security guard took him to the manager's office, where the fun continued. In the office he sat with his feet up on the desk, eating a candy bar, as if he didn't have a care in the world. That was, until, his parents came running into the office.

"We've been looking all over for you!" they said.

When the boy saw the fear on his parents' faces and heard the concern in their voices, his smile transformed to tears. He didn't realize he was lost until he was found.

Jesus often compared us to sheep, which doesn't seem that significant, until I realized that, besides being smelly creatures, sheep aren't very smart. Sheep need a shepherd, not vice versa.

Sheep would get lost, or eaten, without the guidance and protection of a shepherd.

In this passage, Jesus is being criticized by the Pharisees for eating with "sinners." Jesus didn't isolate himself in an air-conditioned sanctuary surrounded with Italian stained glass, not just because these weren't extant at this time, but because that wasn't his style. Jesus loved people and he made a point of being with people—all people—even those who were so good at sin they were given the title, "sinners."

By way of explanation to the Pharisees and illumination to his disciples, Jesus starts telling a story about a wayward sheep. He tells the story of a shepherd who has a hundred sheep, but one wanders away, so he leaves the ninety-nine in an open country . . . and searches for the lost sheep until he finds it. When he finds the lost sheep he puts it on his shoulders, brings it home, and then throws a party.

A party? For a sheep? Doesn't this seem a little irrational? It was only a sheep. Who throws a party for a mangy, smelly, stupid sheep?

The answer: Jesus. If walking this Path with God has taught us anything, it has taught us that Jesus loves people and will not rest until every lost person is found. He longs to put us on his shoulders and carry us home. He can't wait to throw a party celebrating our return. Jesus loves us. Jesus loves you and will do whatever it takes to find you.

Trust me. I know from experience. The second he heard, "Would the father of a lost eight-year-old boy named Arron please come to claim him?" Jesus came running to find me. And when I saw his face, I knew everything was going to be OK.

—Arron Chambers

Spiritual Lessons in Action

Think about what it would be like to be lost in this world without any real hope. Do something today to help one lost person to know that things are going to be OK.

Buried

By Jason B. Miner

Not that I have already obtained all this, or have already been made perfect, but I press on to take hold of that for which Christ Jesus took hold of me. Brothers, I do not consider myself yet to have taken hold of it. But one thing I do: Forgetting what is behind and straining toward what is ahead, I press on toward the goal to win the prize for which God has called me heavenward in Christ Jesus.

—PHILIPPIANS 3:12—14

It was an early Friday morning in Iowa. I had just gotten off from the night shift at the steel frame factory where I worked. I took deliberate, intent footsteps, thinking about what the evening had in store, and then remembered all that had been done to prepare for this moment. I got into my old Ford truck and turned the key. The truck jumped to life as I shifted into first. I was smiling about the future as I drove home that day, but lingering in the past. The past was not done yet, which would actually make it the present. I guess it was one of those in-between times when you're just waiting to wrap things up to move on—it's unnamed, exciting, and sad.

When I pulled into the driveway and turned off the truck, I sat for a while and listened to the engine cool. I looked around at the place, which I had called home for the last three years. It was a small piece of acreage surrounded by plow land as far as the eye could see. It had an old two-story house, a little red barn that was leaning to one side, and several outbuildings in need of paint. It definitely wasn't beautiful, but I loved this place. The sadness of the end filled me. I knew I didn't have time right now to reflect, but I just couldn't help myself. I realized that I needed to get everything in order; otherwise the end would be forgotten.

I opened the truck door and felt the creak echo in my ears. Everything was slow and purposeful this morning. It made me realize how old this time had become; it truly was time to move on. I went to my little garage to find a shovel. The sun was coming in through the half-open door, and as I peered in, it was as if I could see my friends' faces in the flecks of dust glimmering in the new morning light. *Sweet dreams of old*, I thought, as I slid the door open and no one was there. I shook off my feelings and saw the shovel in the corner behind the old stove. I walked over to it, thinking of what it symbolized and wondering where this was all going.

From the garage I went to the house to check on my dog. He was a big black dog with sincere eyes. Even as a puppy he had always seemed serious. Because of those eyes he had been christened with the name Truth. He was a good dog, but lately he seemed to know something was coming. On this morning he just looked at me standing there with my shovel and turned around to go back in the house. *Such a serious puppy*, I thought, but I knew that he wanted no part of what was going to happen. I wanted him to come with me, but I couldn't force him, so I just shrugged my shoulders and headed for the northwest corner of my property.

My route took me by the fire pit, and here I stopped for a moment's revelry. It was here that my friends and I had spent many evenings talking about the whole of the world we knew. Our thoughts were huge in those flames and flickering lights. We were conquering the world's problems—if only they would listen.

To culminate those evenings' activities, sometimes we would snag old couches from the trash. We would stack them high and let them burn as we danced around. I looked into the ashes and saw the springs still in there from the last such outing. I knew that soon I would need to clean that up. Soon but not right now.

I came to the corner of my property and crawled over the old broken barbed-wire fence that separated my land from the farmer's plow land. It was early June, and the fields had been recently planted. The corn was just beginning to show. I looked out over the new life and thought about the next chapter in mine, and then remembered that this one still needed to be closed. I put my shovel on my shoulder and began to walk a half mile through the springtime fields.

My destination was not new, but my purpose was. I kept trying to think slowly and record how I felt, but my thoughts became uncontrollable as I reached the top of the hill, marking the halfway point. Three years earlier was the first time I had taken this walk. It had been with three of my close friends. That first time was in the middle of the night in January. The air was shattering every breath at ten degrees below zero. The reason we went out that night was because of a lie, well, partly because of a lie.

Earlier that evening we were talking about the secrets of the world. The conversation brought to my mind a dream I'd recently had, but when I told them about it, I told it as truth.

I painted the picture of this exact walk I was on now and how when I got to the top of this hill, I saw a point where the uniformity of the field was broken up by two fences coming together, making a 90-degree angle. In this angle there was a patch of trees. To the left was a mess of broken gnarled trees, and to the right were young little trees, but in the center of these two points was a beautiful mature tree that looked like a "Y." I told my friends that I had climbed up in the middle of the tree and felt a sudden peace. It seemed that anything that wasn't resolved I could just give away here, and not be bothered by anymore. I told them this as if it were the truth, but it was just a dream. I had never even set foot out in this area.

My friends were excited about such a strange place and they wanted to go there. No matter how cold it was, they wanted to see it that night. They were so enthusiastic that I had become excited to go as well. I figured when we got there and nothing was as I said it would be, we could all enjoy a good laugh, and I would tell them it was just a dream. It was on that night when we reached the hill—where I now stood—that I realized something strange was in the works. I looked at it now just as amazed as on that night, still not quite understanding what it was—just that it was still really here: the fence, the trees, and the center tree in the shape of a "Y." It was such an unexplainable moment but it seemed to centralize something inside of us—something spiritual, and for this we were starved.

Over the next three years, we told many people about this place, and all of our close friends would end up taking the walk with us. It was not a cult; we weren't worshiping the tree; instead, it was just a mystery that we all hungered for. As I looked at it again, I still couldn't believe it was there. But it was. We had named the spot "The Closure Tree," and I knew that this was going to be my final closure here.

I picked up the shovel on which I'd been leaning and began to finish my walk. At the tree, I searched for a long time, looking for the perfect spot. When I felt I had found it, I began to dig. The ground was soft from the spring rains and made shoveling hard, but I continued to work the hole until it was four feet deep by two feet wide by three feet long. I stepped back and looked at it and told myself it was deep enough to hold the end.

When I was done I set the shovel by the tree and walked back to the house. Truth was waiting for me. I could see his eyes were full of questions. I just patted him on the head and said, "I don't know, old boy. We'll see how it goes."

It was about 10:00 A.M., and I needed some sleep, so Truth and I clambered up the stairs, and I fell into bed as Truth found some comfort by my side. I lay there for a while, taking in every moment I could of the last three years, and then, exhausted from the emotions of the morning, I rolled over and went to sleep.

I awoke in the evening and went downstairs. In the middle of my living room was a plastic tub I had purchased a few days before. I pulled the lid off and looked inside at the emptiness; soon it would be full. It would be filled with the last three years of our lives. I went over to my bookshelf, pulled down a worn-out poetry book, and thumbed through its pages, reading the poems that my friends and I had marked and read aloud to each other over the years. This would be the last night for this book; I felt the cover and traced the lines of titles with my fingers before finally placing it in the bottom of the tub. I looked again at the tub and wondered what the rest of the group would bring. It's funny how big the world can look when you stare into the sky; then, at times like this, it can be encapsulated into a small plastic tub.

The group started to show up before the last of the light had left the sky. It was evident that everybody was wondering what everyone else had brought for this special evening. I decided it was time to put Truth in the house once again. He didn't even look at me, just went inside and walked away.

Outside the group had assembled, and we were ready to go to the tree. There were twelve of us. We had no method to what we were doing, so I suggested that we go to the tree and put our items in the tub when we got there.

We walked in a hushed stroll. Nobody really knew what to say because I don't think there was anything to say.

It was almost finished now. At the top of the hill I stopped and peered into the darkness to see if the tree was there—half expecting it to have disappeared, but there it was. I could see the silhouette of the fence and trees. This was it, and we were at the end.

As we arrived at the spot, everyone stopped and took notice of the dark.

It looked like a grave—and truth be told—it was.

I opened the tub, and we went over the pieces being placed inside. Some people had written letters for us to read when we came back someday; others had mementos from old beat-up cars. One of my friends had written down the lyrics to the song "American Pie," with a brief description of what the symbolism of that song meant. One friend put a VHS tape in that was titled *1987 World Series.* I put in the book of poetry with two bottles of wine, and then we taped the tub shut and put it down in the hole.

At this point we all wanted something to be said but nothing could be said—it was over. One by one, my friends began to walk back. None of us went back together. Not that we were not still friends; instead, we were going our separate ways.

In two months my life was going to change drastically: my house would be sold, my beloved dog Truth would be gone (he was hit by a car at the end of my parents' driveway), and I would be on my way to Europe to search for meaning under the sun. My friends had their own searches on their own roads. It's a moment in time—like childhood or high school—it doesn't go on forever. Our moment was done and, as the last of my friends left the tree, I began to shovel the dirt over the tub.

John Steinbeck, at the beginning of his book *East of Eden* (New York, Penguin Publishers, 1952), writes to a friend about a box—much like our plastic tub. He writes, "Well here's your box. Nearly everything I have is in it, and it is not full. Pain and excitement are in it, and feeling good or bad and evil thoughts and good thoughts—the pleasure of design and the indescribable joy of creation. And on top of these are all the gratitude and love I have for you. And still the box is not full." My friends, still, our box is not full.

† *The Pastor Says* . . .

Traveling with four little children is always an adventure filled with laughter, singing, tears, napping, smells (good and bad), and questions. The most popular being "Are we there yet?"

My eldest son, Levi, is the chief inquisitor. He just likes to know where we are in relation to our destination, so, about every fifteen minutes he'll ask, "Are we there yet?"

When he questions, I don't feel defensive, as if he's wondering if I'm lost, or on my way to being so. No, not at all; I know he trusts me. Levi just has the "can't hardlies."

You know what those are, don't you? The "can't hardlies" are an overwhelming set of feelings that keep the feet moving, the heart racing, and the mind working. The "can't hardlies" usually show up on Christmas Eve, at the gate outside of a theme park, right before a birthday party, and during the last hour of a long trip (or the first hour in Levi's case).

The "can't hardlies" appear when a person "can't hardly" wait for something to happen. So, when Levi asks, I—knowing that he just has a case of the "can't hardlies"—simply reassure him, "No, we're not there yet."

This is exactly what the Apostle Paul is doing in Philippians 3:12–14. He's reminding the Christians in Philippi that they are not "there" yet. None of us are, so we press on and don't quit, until we are "there," because "there" is going to be amazing. When we reach the end of this life, if we have been faithful to God, then we will arrive at the destination of all destinations: Heaven.

Not only is it attainable, it is worth attaining. Detroit is attainable, but I'm yet to be convinced that it is worth attaining, so I'd have to be convinced it's worth sacrificing to get there.

Heaven is worth everything, and we must be willing to sacrifice anything to get there, so Paul challenges us to forget "what is behind" and strain "toward what is ahead" (Phil. 3:13). And, although, we're at the end of our shared journey with God, we are not there yet. We must keep moving forward, so we must leave some things behind.

There are some things we need to bury and leave behind at the base of the tree on which Jesus died.

We need to bury our sins.

We need to bury our insecurities.

We need to bury our fears.

We need to bury our doubts.

We need to bury our pain.

We need to bury anything that might keep us from reaching our destination and walk away from the tree with the "can't hardlies."

No, we aren't there yet.

We must press on.

We must not quit.

We must realize that we are not fighting for victory, but fighting with victory—the battle is already won.

Our faithfulness, our sacrifice, our suffering will all be rewarded, and when we finally arrive at home, Truth will meet us at the door.

—Arron Chambers

Spiritual Lessons in Action

Get a box and fill it with things you need to bury. Get a sheet of paper and list those things that God has forgiven you of, but you have yet to forget. Fold it up and place it in the box. Are there any items that represent mistakes, poor choices, unhealthy relationships, abuse, or anything else that you need to leave behind? Put these in the box with the list and then get a shovel. Find a good spot, bury the box, say a prayer, and have a wondrous day.

About the Editor and Contributors

Arron Chambers is on the preaching team at Christ's Church in Jacksonville, Florida. He is also an adjunct professor at Florida Christian College, a contributing editor of *The Christian Standard,* the president and founder of Tri Life, Inc., a consultant for Creative Training Solutions, a competitive age-group triathlete, an inspirational speaker who speaks to thousands of people each year, the husband of a wonderful woman, and the father of four beautiful kids. He is also the author of *Running on Empty: Life Lessons to Refuel Your Faith* (2005) and *Remember Who You Are* (2007). You can find out more information about Arron's ministry at *www.arronchambers.com.*

Dr. Kimberly Boyd, originally from Atlanta, Georgia, has been a certified teacher since 1987, and has taught in Georgia and Florida public schools. She holds a bachelor's degree in elementary and special education from Georgia Southern College, a master's degree in special education and in emotional disturbances and emotional disorders from West Georgia College, and a doctorate in education leadership from the University of Central Florida. She and her husband, Philip, have two elementary-school-aged children, Keith and Madeline.

Molly Noble Bull, a pro-life Southern Baptist, has published inspirational Christian novels, including *For Always* and *The Rogue's Daughter* (a historical), published in 1986, and *Brides and Blessings*, published in 1999. *The Winter Pearl,* Molly's long inspirational historical, was published in November 2004 and reviewed by Christian Book Previews. Molly's newest novel, *Sanctuary,* is set to be released in

September 2007. Molly writes for the Christian market only and her Web site is *http://mollybull.theaardvark.com.*

Susan Page Davis is a Maine native. She and her husband, Jim, have been married thirty years and have six children, ages 11 to 28. They are active in a small, independent Baptist church. Susan has authored several Christian historical romance novels and has published short stories in the romance, humor, and mystery fields. She is a homeschooling mother and news writer.

Tamara J. Davis lives in Jacksonville, Florida, with her husband, Terry, and their four children, Madison, Josiah, Sawyer, and Jaden. She currently serves in the children's ministry at Christ's Church Mandarin as a Sunday morning storyteller and comic cohost. She loves sharing God's word with kids in a fun and exciting way. Tammy has performed in and written several dramas for church use and spent some time performing improv comedy at SAK Comedy Lab in Orlando.

Laurie Alice Eakes says that from the time her parents read to her throughout her childhood, novels, essays, and poetry have been a part of her life. An English teacher in a Christian school, Laurie Alice has seen many articles and short stories published, and recently sold her first full-length novel. A graduate of Asbury College and Seton Hall University, she lives in Virginia with her husband, two yellow Labradors, and a cat who keeps her desk chair warm in the rare times it's vacated.

David Faust serves as president of Cincinnati Christian University and executive editor of *The Lookout*, a national magazine for Christian families. A minister for more than thirty years, David has led growing churches in New York, Cincinnati, and Indianapolis, and he has authored or coauthored hundreds of published articles and twelve books, including *Taking Truth Next Door, Faith Under Fire,* and *Married for Good.* David and his wife Candy have three grown children, a son-in-law, and two granddaughters.

Kathleen Fuller is the author of two novellas, five novels, and numerous nonfiction articles. She has appeared on the radio programs *Janet Parshall's America* and *Water Through the Word.* Her latest novel, *Special Assignment,* was released in October 2005, and is available from Avalon Books. Currently a special education teacher, Kathleen lives on a small farm in Geneva, Ohio, with her husband, James, and their three children.

Kenneth R. Funk is an executive with a global theme park and entertainment company based in Orlando, Florida; serves on the board of directors of the University of Central Florida Christian Campus Fellowship; is an elder at Southside Christian Church in Orlando; has consulted, led seminars, and facilitated workshops in the areas of business development, staffing and hiring, and customer service; and has led numerous Bible-based series for practical living. He is the husband of a beautiful wife, and the father of two great sons.

Leigh-Angela Holbrook has worked in ministries with youth, education, worship, and women's studies for twenty years, and has worked as a team builder and speaker at various events. She's married to Jeff Holbrook, a pilot for FedEx, and has a fifteen-year-old son, Hunter. She lives just outside of Houston, Texas.

Marc Imboden is a singer-songwriter based in Indianapolis who leads people in worship and tours with his band, Year's Wages. You might know him from the song "You are Holy/Prince of Peace" as recorded by more than two hundred artists. He and his wife, Amy, have one son, Nash, and another baby on the way. Marc has two CDs available, *Come to the Table* and *Drive*.

Kim Jackson is a writer, speaker, and found-object artist. Known as the "Kimmunicator," her passion is to creatively communicate the love of God in written form, spoken word, and created object. Kim travels extensively and humor and creativity are the hallmarks of her presentations. Kim has been published in a variety of periodicals, and is currently working on a book titled *Totally Scary Girls for God: Forty Frighteningly Fab Females of Faith.* Kim can be contacted at *Kimagine320@yahoo.com*, or through her Web site, *www.Kimmunicator.com*.

Dr. Rebecca Price Janney is a theologically trained historian and the author of fifteen books including *Great Women in American History, Great Stories in American History, Harriet Tubman,* and two young-adult series. She began writing professionally at age fourteen. A graduate of Lafayette College, Princeton, and Biblical Seminaries, she enjoys sharing with readers the marvelous acts of God throughout history. Rebecca lives in suburban Philadelphia with her husband and son.

Paul "Doc" Johnson was born in 1924 in Bath, Maine. A decorated fighter pilot in World War II and Korea, he was senior command pilot, colonel, air group commander, combat ace, and an escaped prisoner of war in Korea. He retired in 1975 as a chief engineer at General Motors Corporation and holds B.S., M.S., and Ph.D. degrees in mechanical engineering. Paul resides in Orlando, Florida, with his wife Peggy. He is an elder and former board chairman at First Christian Church of Winter Park, Florida. He is now the assistant to the president at Florida Christian College, where he specializes in estate planning, which includes wills and trusts.

Serenity Johnson was born in Punta Gorda, Florida. She and her husband Dan, whom she met during a choir trip in college, are enjoying their new life as a married couple and are excited to see what God has in store for their future, which is wholly undecided. She and Dan hope to move somewhere exotic, like Tallahassee or Cincinnati, or Tokyo, to eat lots of sushi.

Timothy W. Jones is a comedian. In the early years, comedy for Tim was falling out of chairs in math class, or drawing goofy likenesses of various study-hall teachers in the blue-collar steel town of Latrobe, Pennsylvania. Eventually, Tim crawled down out of the trees, learned to make fire, and evolved into a bona fide funny guy. His early career was spent as a church teen counselor and as a history teacher, two professions crying out for comedy. Today, Tim travels around the country performing at various locations and, as a squeaky-clean comic, his humor runs between "cerebral" for college crowds to "gross" for junior-high audiences. And he's able to clear clogged breathing passages in as fast as fifteen seconds. Tim's Web site is *www.steptwin.com.*

Jason B. Miner grew up in Manly, Iowa, dreaming of one day seeing the world. Little by little, this dream has been achieved, and it is his desire to share the experiences from these travels in writing. He has two books that he is currently pursuing publication on, and a loving wife that is a true support. He is enrolled at Florida Christian College, working toward a bachelor of arts in preaching, and hopes to be in the mission field in Bolivia in three years.

Paula Munier is a veteran writer and editor who believes in everyday miracles, Pinewood Derby and otherwise. She lives in a lakeside cottage on Boston's South Shore with her son Michael, two dogs, and a cat.

Tamela Hancock Murray is an award-winning, bestselling author of nineteen romance novels and ten novellas for the Christian market. She is also the author of three Bible trivia books for children and three more for adults. Tamela is an agent for Hartline Literary Agency. She enjoys living in northern Virginia with her husband of more than twenty years and two beautiful daughters. To learn more about her life and work, please visit *www.tamelahancockmurray .com.*

Andrew Peterson, a singer-songwriter, has been telling stories through music for the last ten years. His most recent album, *The Far Country,* was released in 2005 to critical acclaim. Andrew feels God's pleasure when he's on stage and has traveled through all fifty states and Europe, but his favorite place in the world is by the fireplace at home in Nashville, Tennessee, with his wife and three kids.

Melissa Reyes is currently a senior at the University of Florida, pursuing a bachelor of music degree in piano performance, with an outside emphasis on history. Her current internship with UF ministry Christian Campus House has allowed her to participate in various mission trips to England, Austria, and Tanzania. She also recently coreleased a CD entitled *Intricate* through Justice Road Productions, a record label owned by Desire Street Ministries of New Orleans. For more information about the CD and this urban ministry, visit *www.justiceroad.com.*

Kimberly Ripley is a freelance writer from Portsmouth, New Hampshire. The author of six books, she is grateful to God for the blessings of her husband, five children, daughter-in-law, and many special friends—as well as her love of writing. Visit Kim's Web site at *www.kimberlyripley.writergazette.com.*

Bob Russell became the pastor of Southeast Christian Church in Louisville, Kentucky, at age twenty-two. Thirty-eight years later, that small congregation of 120 members has become one of the largest churches in America, with 20,000 people attending the three worship services every weekend. Bob and his wife, Judy, have two married sons and six grandchildren, with whom they enjoy spending their time. Bob has written over a dozen books; the latest, *The Power of One Another,* was released in 2004. He also has a weekly column in *The Lookout.* A highly respected speaker, Bob is heard weekly on *The Living Word* and he inspires listeners to consider Biblical truths as they relate to life in contemporary culture.

Kim Vogel Sawyer, a Kansas resident, is fond of "c" words like children, cats, and chocolate. Kim stays active in her church, teaching adult Sunday School, singing in the choir, and being a "ding-a-ling" (bell-choir participant). She and her husband, Don, have three daughters and two grandsons. She welcomes visitors to her Web site at *www.KimVogelSawyer.com.*

Twila Sias enjoys life with her husband and sons. She is grateful for the chance to be involved in the developing lives of students at Florida Christian College in Kissimmee, Florida, where she has taught for the last twenty-five years in the education program. Though a Floridian for over thirty years, she recalls with fondness her roots in southern Illinois that have shaped her life.

Robin Sigars is a director of conferences for the nationally known organization Christ In Youth. Robin travels around the world each year speaking to thousands of teens and adults about their relationship with Jesus, their parents, and their children, and about how to work with teens. Robin and his wife, Jayme, have seven children. Christ In Youth is a parachurch organization, planning conferences and weekend events for children through teenagers; its Web site is *www.ciy.com*. Robin's e-mail address is *Robin.Sigars@ciy.com*.

John H. Smith grew up in Elizabethton, Tennessee and earned two degrees from Cincinnati Christian University. He has held ministries in Kentucky, Indiana, Florida, and Tennessee. He has also conducted numerous revivals and has been known for his Sermons in Song, which are sermons interspersed with gospel songs. He has contributed articles to *The Restoration Herald* and currently is serving as minister at the East Side Christian Church in Elizabethton, Tennessee. John and his wife, Mary, have four children and twelve grandchildren. All of their children are in some form of Christian ministry.

C. Robert Wetzel currently serves as the president of Emmanuel School of Religion in Johnson City, Tennessee. He held an eleven-year ministry as principal of Springdale College in Birmingham, England. Prior to that, he served Milligan College as a philosophy professor for nineteen years, six of which included serving as academic dean. He is a graduate of Midwest Christian College (now Ozark Christian College), Fort Hays State University, and the University of Nebraska, where he received a Ph.D. degree. From 2004 to 2008, he will serve as president of the World Convention. He and his wife Bonnie have been married for fifty-two years and are the parents of two grown daughters.

Paul S. Williams is the president of Orchard Group (formerly Go Ye Chapel Mission), a New York–based church-planting organization that grows larger congregations in strategic and challenging environments. More information about the organization can be found at *www.orchardgroup.org*. Paul is the author of *Laughter, Tears, and In-Between: Soulful Stories for the Journey* (2001). He speaks at numerous national and regional conventions and conferences, and serves as an adjunct seminary instructor. Paul is also a board member and on-air host with the Worship Network, seen nightly on over seventy PAX-TV stations throughout the United States. He also serves as editor-at-large of *Christian Standard* magazine.

Leslie Wood has a degree in Christian education. She married Shan Wood in 1988, and is now in full-time ministry with her husband in Orlando, Florida. She has worn many hats in her years of ministry, including being a teacher. When her twins were born, she made the commitment to stay home full-time, and after adding a beautiful girl to the family, decided to be not only a mom but also a home-school teacher! In her spare time she also works with the church music teams, children's choir, and ladies' Bible study.